W9-CDF-095

Reading the Classics
and *Paradise Lost*

Reading the Classics
and *Paradise Lost*

Wᴵʟʟᴵᴀᴍ M. Pᴏʀᴛᴇʀ

University of Nebraska Press
Lincoln and
London

© 1993 by the University of Nebraska Press
All rights reserved
Manufactured in the United States of America
The paper in this book meets the minimum
requirements of American National Standard for
Information Sciences—Permanence of Paper for
Printed Library Materials,
ANSI Z39.48–1984.

*Library of Congress Cataloging-in-
Publication Data*
Porter, William M. (William Malin), 1951–
Reading the classics and Paradise lost
/ by William M. Porter.
p. cm.
ISBN 0-8032-3706-5 (alk. paper)
1. Milton, John, 1608–1674. Paradise lost.
2. Milton, John, 1608–1674—Knowledge—
Literature. 3. Epic poetry, English—Classical
influences. 4. Classicism—England.
5. Intertextuality. I. Title.
PR3562.P67 1993
821'.4—dc20 92-24241
CIP

Whom the grand foe with scornful eye askance
Thus answered. Ill for thee, but in wished hour
Of my revenge, first sought for thou return'st
From flight, seditious angel, to receive
Thy merited reward, the first assay
Of this right hand provoked, since first that tongue
Inspired with contradiction durst oppose
A third part of the gods, in synod met
Their deities to assert, who while they feel
Vigor divine within them, can allow
Omnipotence to none. . . .

                   —*Paradise Lost* 6.149–59

Contents

Preface

The ambivalence of focus suggested by the conjunction in my title—*Reading the Classics* and "*Paradise Lost*"—is deliberate. *Paradise Lost* is constantly in view in the pages that follow, as no single classical text is. But my interest in the classics is not subordinated to my interest in Milton's poem. On the contrary, I make my professional home in a classics program rather than in an English department, and as I puzzled over Milton's rich allusions to certain classical texts, I tried to take them seriously in themselves and not just to look for whatever Milton seemed to be pointing at. This is, I believe, what Milton wants of us, but it does make life difficult sometimes. This study, unlike most previous studies of Milton's classicism in this century, is not intended to be remedial.

Of course, the nature of literary scholarship in the late days of this millenium makes it virtually impossible for scholars— even if they had his native gifts—to acquire Milton's intimate knowledge of the all of the more important ancient and modern literatures, in the original languages. Recognizing that the classics are not the common currency among educated readers that they once were, I have tried to make that which is relevant in the ancient texts as accessible as possible: my references to the classical texts are often fairly explicit, and translations— my own, unless otherwise noted—are provided in the body of the text for all Greek and Latin quotations. But I have tried even harder not to minimize the richness and complexity of meaning that I think Milton himself is drawing upon. *Paradise Lost*'s engagement with its classical pre-texts is not a baroque embellishment, but rather a matter of radical—one might say *genetic*—significance to the poem. And while I do not subscribe to the vulgar view that poems mean whatever we want them to, still, it strikes me that Milton has not wholly determined the meaning of this engagement. Instead he has made it contingent upon the reader's own understanding of the classics. In other words, he has put upon us readers a burden that is almost too much for us to bear. The best we can do, then, is to read the ancient texts that Milton invokes as honestly and fairly as we read *Paradise Lost* itself; I think it will be apparent that this best, inadequate as it may be, has seldom been done before. I have in one way or another taken into account everything that seems important to me, but the subject is in its nature inexhaustible and my sense of what is important does not derive from reasoned judgment so much as my inevitably partial perception of what is there. Accordingly, I do not pretend to be definitive or comprehensive; in fact, I have worked hard to avoid giving that impression. It would have been easier to write a book twice as long.

I apologize for those of my failings as an amateur Miltonist that I have not been able to uncover and remedy before publication, and I beg that the professionals grant me a little indulgence. I would ask for a little indulgence from my colleagues in classics as well. I largely overlook current scholastic controversies regarding the interpretation of the classics. This is not because I am only concerned with how the texts were read by Milton in the seventeenth century—quite the contrary. But our scholastic controversies are often parochially historical in a different way. What we as scholars know (or think we know), for example, about how Homer's poetry was experienced in archaic Greece by its original auditors, is distinguishable from what we experience as ordinary readers. (I submit that the "ordinary reader" is no more hypothetical a construct than the "scholar.") I do take into account in a general way some apparent advances in recent criticism, such as our enhanced awareness of the anti-imperial undertow of the *Aeneid*, but not in order to fault Milton. How Milton the scholar read the classics is seldom an issue in what follows. I will try to demonstrate instead that Milton the poet found a way to finesse his own limited reading and play against his allusive pre-texts in a manner that is as durably interesting as any other dimension of his poetry.

THE Hesiodic and Horatian parts of chapter 2 originally appeared as, respectively, "A View from 'th' Aonian Mount': Hesiod and Milton's Critique of the Classics," *Classical and Modern Literature* 3 (1982): 5–23, and "Milton and Horace: The Post-Bellum Muse," *Comparative Literature* 35 (1983): 351–61. I wish to thank *CML*, Inc., and the editors of *Comparative Literature* for permission to reprint.

The idea for this book first came to me in the early 1980s when I was a Mellon Fellow in Renaissance Studies at Brandeis University. My debts to the Andrew W. Mellon Foundation and to my institutional host, Brandeis University (in particular, to the programs in Classical Studies and English), are incalculable. I should also mention Harvard University, the University of Texas, and Rice University, which gave me easy access to their collections of rare books and whose librarians were all most helpful. The University of Houston supported me in this project in the beginning, middle, and end: back in the early stages of my research, with a summer grant; at the end of the

project, with a subvention to assist with publication; and in
the middle—this seems to deserve mention—by not forcing
me to rush this book into print prematurely in order to meet
a deadline for tenure.

Finally, I want to express my gratitude publicly to a few
people who have given me special encouragement and assistance during various stages of this project: Virginia Leon de
Viveró and James Loyd of *CML*; W. R. Johnson of the University of Chicago, my old advisers and friends, D. S. Carne-
Ross and William G. Riggs of Boston University and William
Mullen of Bard College; Harold Jones of Syracuse University, my former chairman here in Houston; and, not least, my
present colleagues, James Houlihan and Dora C. Pozzi.

Introduction

Does *Paradise Lost* contain or advance an interpretation of the classics? So my predecessors in this field of critical inquiry have often thought. In fact, it has been alleged by two of the major expositors of Milton's classical allusions in this century that *Paradise Lost* does more than adumbrate a general interpretation of this or that work or of the classics generally: it actually constitutes a detailed commentary. Davis P. Harding finds Milton dropping little glosses everywhere, but sees one specific text as Milton's principal concern. "*Paradise Lost* remains, when all is said and done, the finest commentary on Virgil's *Aeneid* ever written," says Harding in the concluding sentence of *The Club of Hercules,* long the prime authority on the subject of Milton and the classics.[1] Not content to view Milton as an explicator of Vergil alone, Francis C. Blessington expands the claim to include the two poems of Homer. In the introduction to *"Paradise Lost" and the Classical Epic,* defending his decision to focus on the classical texts exclusively and to disregard the interpretative tradition through which Milton must have viewed them, Blessington says, "*Paradise Lost* is Milton's own commentary on these classical texts." Later, in the first paragraph of his first chapter, Blessington insists on the scholastic metaphor, saying that "Milton intended his poem to be read as a gloss" upon the *Iliad,* the *Odyssey,* and the *Aeneid.*[2]

The mechanism whereby Milton ties his "commentary" to
its subject texts is, of course, the verbal allusion. But as a commentative device, allusion is a trickier thing than the more
conventional line note. An allusion is, after all, a latent comment, not an explicit one, and it requires the mediation of
scholars such as Harding and Blessington to be brought to
light. The situation soon becomes depressingly Alexandrian:
commentary begets and then becomes dependent upon meta-
commentary, so that we lose almost completely the sense of
direct contact with a poetic original. This should, I believe,
create more anxiety than it seems to have done, particularly
because there is evidence aplenty that the meta-commentators
are not reliable.

I will deal with this in more detail in chapter 1, but the slip-
periness of allusion can be suggested here by a single example.
In Milton's description of Satan, that

> he above the rest
> In shape and gesture proudly eminent
> Stood like a tower,
>
> (*Paradise Lost* 1.589–91)

Davis Harding sees an allusion to Vergil's description of Turnus,

> ipse inter primos praestanti corpore Turnus
> uertitur arma tenens et toto uertice supra est.
>
> (*Aeneid* 7.783–84)

Harding offers the translation of Mackail:

> Himself too amongst the foremost, splendid in
>   beauty of body,
> Turnus moves armed and towers a whole head
>   over all.

Says Harding, "It seems probable that Virgil's second line suggested the simile 'Stood like a Tow'r.'"[3] But no line or word of Vergil's could suggest this particular connection to Harding. There is in the Latin no "tower" (*turris*—no cognate verb), only "supra est," meaning literally "he is above," "he is higher." Is this an allusion—that is, a significant verbal link between Milton's text and Vergil's? I think not; I suspect instead that Harding was looking more closely at Mackail's English than at Vergil's Latin. But I hesitate to give an impression of overconfidence. There *is* a vague similarity in the contexts of the two passages. And height is a generic characteristic of epic or martial heroes, as even the Bible acknowledges when it draws attention to Goliath's or Saul's height. One contributor to the first variorum edition of Milton's poetry (1749), Bishop Stillingfleet, refers to Homer's description of Ajax as ἔξοχος Ἀργείων κεφαλήν τε καὶ εὐρέας ὤμους (*Iliad* 3.227: "Preeminent among the Argives with his head and broad shoulders"). This is no closer than "supra est," and yet we can be fairly confident that Stillingfleet was thinking of the original. The editor of the second variorum (1809), the Reverend Henry Todd, refers to Dante, *Purgatorio* 5.14, "Sta, come torre ferma." After seeing even the best of the allusion-mongers ply their trade in this fashion, readers interested in interpreting Milton's poetry may be forgiven if they feel an urge to move on to something more important.

I draw my reader's attention to this scene of confusion not to belittle Harding's small Latin,[4] but to suggest that mere verbal similarity is not the real issue here at all. Harding has ulterior motives. He sees an allusion here because he believes a priori that Milton wants to associate Satan with Turnus. If verbal similarity were all that mattered, Harding might have mentioned as well *Aeneid* 11.683 ("uertitur in mediis et toto uertice supra est"), which is almost identical to the line in book 7 to which he draws attention. But 11.683 describes one Ornytus, a minor Trojan victim of Camilla's killing spree: not nearly as sexy an association. The idea that Milton's classical allusions are designed to associate his chief characters (Satan, Adam, Eve, and a few others) with the principals of pagan epic has been fundamental to most studies of Milton's classicism. It is a crude hermeneutic, enabling critics, after they have found or invented an allusion, to make some hay with it. I have never read a fair argument of this point, but the critics evidently presume that Milton's values are radically antithetical to those of classical epic—as if the values of Homer and Vergil were identical! This leads typically to the claim that Milton has one way or another vanquished the classical tradition.

Francis C. Blessington's 1979 study represented a big advance over previous work because it saw that an association of, for example, Satan with Turnus is as likely to discredit Satan as Turnus. But Blessington, too, is tendentious, even as he strives to be balanced:

> In the classical epic, man is so much the measure of all things that when Odysseus was offered immortality by Calypso, he refused it (*Od.* V, 203–24). The gods of Homer and Virgil do not live the vital lives of men; the classical epic centered itself, as Greek culture did, on man. Milton reverses this tradition and has put God back in the center of the epic world, although he works within the framework of the classical epic and uses more than he rejects. The Father emerges out of a cloud of classical error and is seen to be the true source of all virtue. Homer and Virgil were not wrong—Homer saw the faults of Achilles as well as anyone—but they did not see far enough into the theological workings of the world.[5]

If we are looking primarily for information about the "theological workings of the world," we should be reading Milton's *De Doctrina Christiana* instead of his *Paradise Lost*; and besides, as I shall suggest later, I have my doubts about whether Milton's progress is real. In any case, outside Blessington (who characterizes the classical poets as admirably pious but benighted), the picture usually drawn pits a decrepit band of pagans against the vigorous modern, so that it can be said of Milton, as he himself says of the Son, that even in victory "half his strength he put not forth." My own view is that Milton is a great poet, but not a savior. If Vergil's epic is "secondary," Milton's is arguably "tertiary," but it is quite possible to see in this sequence not so much a progress as a decline.

If Milton's poem does in some way constitute a commentary or even an interpretation of classical epic, then I fear that we who speak for the classics must reject it as silly or, at best, quaint. It may be that the general indifference nowadays to the classical dimension of *Paradise Lost* reflects not only the increasing unfamiliarity of Milton's readers with his authoritative pre-texts, but equally the presumption, by those who are not ignorant of those pre-texts, that Milton's critique of the classics is impertinent or simply unimportant. Ironically, the more affirmative picture of the classics found in Blessington particularly, while it avoids the faults of the earlier anticlassical theory, is in some ways even more pernicious, because it renders both the classics *and* Milton uninteresting: the classics because they are somehow "wrong," and Milton because his poem is now just a new version of an old product, heroic epic, improved by the addition of (as we would say today) "the secret ingredient—Xianity!"

I submit that Harding, Blessington, and others have it wrong. On the contrary, *Paradise Lost* is not a commentary. It does not advance an interpretation of the classics generally or of any classical work in particular and the suggestion that it does seems to reflect a misunderstanding of the nature of poetry. As W. R. Johnson puts it,

> Poets are not theologians or philosophers or historians. They do not quite think thoughts, they do not quite deliver messages. They *see* their own feelings and the feelings of their contemporaries, and from what they see they fashion dreams of reality.[6]

Milton may leap to mind as an exception, along with Lucretius and Dante. But Johnson is thinking here of Lucan, who likewise has always seemed a poet with an ideological axe to grind. The issue is exceedingly complex. I doubt that one book, even one much longer than this, could deal adequately with both the theoretical and practical implications, and it is very largely the latter that concern me here. As we will see later in some detail, Milton seems quite clearly to disparage the ancients from time to time. But these facile condemnations hardly constitute an "interpretation." They are, rather, an aspect of Milton's imaginative rhetoric and no more reflect the historic Milton's personal or scholarly views than the gnomic chestnuts scattered throughout Horace's *Satires, Odes,* and *Epistles* represent the final reaches of his own wisdom.

To say that *Paradise Lost* does not itself advance or expound an interpretation of the classics does not mean, however, that the interpretation of the classics is not at issue. Richard J. DuRocher, defending his general disregard of the commentative tradition that brought the classics to Milton, writes:

> The crucial question . . . is how one fiercely independent poet, overtly skeptical of glosses and commentaries, incorporated and adapted the *Metamorphoses* within his epic.[7]

I, too, will say little about the seventeenth century's reading of the classics, but it is not because I suppose Milton's reading somehow transcends time. It is, rather, that Milton's reading is not the issue at all: ours is. DuRocher is quite right to note Milton's Protestant attitude toward commentaries, but I think he misunderstands it or at least misappropriates it to his own use.[8] When Milton in the *De Doctrina Christiana* (1.30) writes in regard to the interpretation of the Bible that "We are expressly forbidden to pay any regard to human traditions, whether written or unwritten," he is using a little Protestant hyperbole. There is no question of Milton's disregarding the prior traditions of commentary, on the Bible or the classics. But Milton's hermeneutic principle is a reflection of the Protestant notion that every Christian must read and interpret Scripture for himself: it is a principle of hermeneutic responsibility. Instead of interpreting the classics for us, *Paradise Lost* does something more interesting, something more challenging as well—something that might even have the potential to be embarrassing: it makes an issue of the reader's own interpretation of the ancient works. If it has failed to do so in this century, I can only suspect it is because increasingly few of Milton's readers have had an interpretation to make an issue of.

This book focuses on the fact that this strategy of engagement with the classics is built around an epic technique that seldom in any particular use extends beyond a single verse: the allusion. In the past, critics have too often decided in advance what Milton's allusions were likely to mean on the basis of their understanding of his general purposes in *Paradise Lost*. I suppose these critics fancied themselves to be "reading the allusions in context." The problem was that the predetermined readings were generally so crude that it took some effort to make them fit the phenomena, but this gave the critics a healthy challenge; and there was no shortage of phenomena, since an ingenious critic could make almost anything look like an allusion. Now the study of Milton's allusions, perhaps the dominant aspect of commentary in the eighteenth century, has not been a major current in the criticism of the twentieth, but those who have worked in this field have spent less time discrediting the claims of their predecessors than they have spent adding to the stockpile of claims. (As I suggested near the start of this introduction, it is devilishly difficult to prove that something is *not* an allusion.) So the impression has inevitablity been created that Milton alludes ubiquitously, almost indiscriminately, to the classics, as well as to the Bible and numerous other prior literatures. Ironically, the results of this "research" have been, I fear, counterproductive. At a time when even well-educated readers have found it increasingly difficult to recognize even the more elementary of these allusions, our growing suspicion that the allusions are largely, if not entirely, decorative has not been allayed by the contrary protestations of the allusion-experts.

The work of these critics has in fact fed these suspicions. The allusions appear to be deictic, to point to something, but earlier critics, because they believed that the meaning of *Paradise Lost* must be self-contained and that therefore it could not really be pointing outside itself to anything important, came to treat the allusions as if they were formal gestures, reflecting gracefully off the classical texts and returning to artful repose on the surface of *Paradise Lost*. I, on the other hand, have tried to take the deictic appearance of Milton's allusions at face value. This has necessitated examining the target texts more closely than previous critics did. I have not presumed that the context of the allusion in Milton determined the meaning, but, on the contrary, have tried to remain open to the possibility that the context of the target text might be critically important. There was no alternative, of course, to examining, one at a time, each of the intertextual links that has been claimed by prior critics or that I felt I might have noticed for myself. This procedure, I must confess, was tedious and usually unrewarding. Again and again I was unable to find much of a point to something that at first looked like a fairly promising intertextual link. But I found a few that were more meaningful than I had expected them to be, and when the dust settled, these few began to look as if they might have been used in deliberate concert. These are at the heart of this book.

In the first chapter, subtitled "Allusion," I make some practical distinctions among the varieties of intertextuality that readers encounter in *Paradise Lost* in order to isolate a particular type of allusion that I dub "critical." A critical allusion is one in which the homologies between source-text (*Paradise Lost*) and target (for example, the *Aeneid*) extend beyond local verbal resemblances to the larger contexts, and in which the relationship of allusive source (the later text) to target (the earlier) is dialectical, that is, the source is aggressively critical of the target, but in a manner that is obviously unfair, so that the reader feels—or at least ought to feel—compelled to speak up on behalf of the target text. I suggest in this first chapter and will go on to demonstrate later that Milton's allusions are rarer than previously thought. But this rareness is crucial to their moment. The view that Milton is engaging the classics in every other line renders the notion of engagement trivial; but the classics do not—could not—respond to Milton's thousand petty acknowledgments.

In the second and third chapters, then, I explicate a handful of these critical allusions. Chapter 2, subtitled "Thought," examines a network of allusions to Hesiod and Horace in the center of *Paradise Lost* that constitutes the core of Milton's

ironic anticlassical argument. Chapter 3, subtitled "Design,"
surveys Milton's allusive engagement with Vergil and suggests
that the *Aeneid* is the most important of Milton's authoritative
pre-texts. Of course, this claim has been made in the past, but
too facilely. I will show that an elaborate pattern of structural
references to the *Aeneid* has been built into *Paradise Lost*, not as
an end in itself, but to provide a more dramatic framework for
a handful of allusions that strike to the heart of both poems.
My main concern is with verbal allusion and its consequences,
and I have tried to avoid the grosser aspects of Milton's relationship to his predecessors, such as genre or convention.[9]
The appendix, which deals with the fact that in its first (1667)
edition, *Paradise Lost* was divided into ten books rather than
twelve, is particularly relevant to the argument of this chapter. The thought and design that chapters 2 and 3 explore are
not so much types of content as dimensions of critical reflection expressed obliquely: it might have been more accurate to
speak of thinking and designing. These processes have an in-
triguing rhetorical life of their own, complementary to the life
of the poem as a whole, but almost independent of it, because
they are so heavily dependent on the life of a variety of alien
texts, Milton's targets.

The fourth and final chapter, subtitled "Language," is at
once the most elementary and the most tentative in the book.
Relinquishing the narrow focus on specific allusions that I
maintained previously, I turn to make a distinction between
literary imitation and true allusion by considering a general
aspect of Milton's allusions that strikes me as profoundly significant, namely, the fact that they are articulated in English
rather than Latin or Greek. My point here is that Milton's allusions always involve translation, and that translation, at least as
practiced by a creative genius, thrives on linguistic difference.

For a point of comparison, I turn here not to Milton's own Latin poetry (most of which seems to me to be remote in spirit from *Paradise Lost*) but to two other texts, one little known, Jacopo Sannazaro's *De Partu Virginis,* and the other virtually unknown, William Dobson's *Paradisus Amissus,* a translation of *Paradise Lost* into Latin. My remarks on Sannazaro do not involve detailed comparison between his work and and Milton's, but I hope their pertinence to the general concerns of the book will be apparent from their placement in the middle of a larger discussion of Dobson.

1

Nec plura adludens:
Allusion

The Difficulty of Attempting to
Isolate Literary Allusions

Literary critical nomenclature provides a variety of terms describing the local association of one work with another: *allusion, reminiscence, borrowing,* and *echo* are the most common. *Allusion* is most often used as a compendiary term, but the variety of terms seems to recognize the possibility of distinctions, for example, between what is and is not an allusion, and between various degrees or kinds of allusive significance. Intertextuality has been the subject of some attention from literary theoreticians in the last few decades, but these theoretical investigations seem to have had little effect on practical criticism. Practical critics apparently are unwilling to surrender the notion that an allusion exists where one can be found; this gives them the greatest liberty and the greatest responsibility. If critical use of the descriptive terms seems often to be rather indiscriminate, that is not surprising. Practical critics are seldom born taxonomists.

Before we can consider the larger aspects of *Paradise Lost*'s relationship to the Greek and Roman classics—thought, design, language—we must isolate the intertextual figure that underpins everything else, allusion. To do this, it will be necessary to discriminate, however tentatively, among the various ways in which *Paradise Lost* points to or associates itself with the classics and the classical world. I will try to show that these distinctions are not so much matters of degree of significance as they are of kind. The proper criterion by which to make these distinctions is not the extent of the resemblance between one passage and another, so much as the nature of its critical or interpretative consequence. The failure of previous critics to make these distinctions has caused Milton's small handful of critically important allusions to become lost in a welter of commentary. It is not my purpose here to suggest that Milton's more minor instances of intertextuality are unimportant. They form the backdrop against which the critical allusions are intended to be displayed. Nevertheless, I submit that the critical allusions are a distinct kind of thing.

What I am concerned with in this chapter may be initially (and awkwardly) described as any association between some aspect of *Paradise Lost* and something that has a prior, knowable existence and meaning outside of Milton's poem, aside from the particulars of human experience that are designated by the ordinary words of the English language. Of course, the complexity of the matter resists even such a fundamental description, with its admittedly and inevitably vague exception ("aside from . . ."). At times the meaning of a passage is direct and simple: "Then when I am thy captive talk of chains" (4.970). Anyone who knows English knows what these words mean. Certain words may be loaded with particular meanings or resonances by the poet, as, for example, the word *fruit,* but do not primarily depend upon any extraordinary extratextual traditions of significance. On the other hand, certain apparently innocent common nouns, such as *light* in the proem to *Paradise Lost,* book 3, do in fact draw upon particular uses by prior authors, including Spenser, Dante, St. John, and St. Augustine, as well as Benedict Pererius on Dionysius the Areopagite, and Marsilio Ficino and the Florentine neo-Platonists.[1] Somewhat different is the significance of apparently simple words that, when put together in a special way, in fact constitute a specific verbal allusion, as, for example, Milton's testimony that he is "smit with the love of sacred song" (3.29), which alludes to Vergil's *ingenti percussus amore* (*Georgics* 2.476: "struck with a great love," viz. of the Muses). These complexities could easily be compounded. All meaning is admittedly extratextual in some way.

Our topic may be more narrowly described then as the significant connections between *Paradise Lost* and the prior learned traditions of Europe, particularly as those traditions are embodied in books. Some of these connections smack of the library, but not of any particular book; these fall easily into categories and present few hermeneutic problems. Such are Milton's displays of erudition—geographical:

> from Paneas the fount of Jordan's flood
> To Beersaba, where the Holy Land
> Borders on Aegypt and the Arabian shore,
>
> (3.535–37)

—astronomical:

> his golden scales, yet seen
> Betwixt Astrea and the Scorpion sign,
>
> (4.997–98)

—and historical:

> Such of late
> Columbus found the American so girt
> With feathered cincture, naked else and wild.
>
> (9.1115–17)

There is no critical difference between the learning displayed (and demanded) by these passages. They simply call for a little knowledge, usually of a sort that in Milton's day, as in our own, is easily gotten out of an encyclopedia. More complex is the interpretation of what might be called doctrinal content. The entire poem may be said to be doctrinal, but the doctrine seems particularly concentrated in certain nodal passages, such as the invocation of light in the proem to book 3, or this passage from book 5:

> Well hast thou taught the way that might direct
> Our knowledge, and the scale of nature set
> From centre to circumference, whereon
> In contemplation of created things
> By steps we may ascend to God. (5.508–12)

Homer, *Iliad* 8.19, and Plato, *Theaetetus* 153c, are the primary sources of the idea here, but its significance in Milton's day was a result of a mass of commentary and development of the idea during the intervening centuries. Milton should not be supposed here to be alluding specifically either to Homer or to Plato.

These doctrinal nodes have a far richer background than the displays of geographical or astronomical knowledge. And yet it should be noted that neither the doctrinal nor the other displays *refer* to anything. They draw upon something that the reader is expected to know, but they do not refer to that something implicitly or explicitly. The hermeneutic motion in the passage quoted above is centripetal, or, we may say, historical: the motion is from Homer, through Plato, to Milton. When Milton writes, "Since God is light," he is not tacitly directing his reader to look again at the neo-Platonist Ficino, a possible source of this passage, from the new perspective of Milton's use and implied interpretation of him. On the other hand, when he writes, "In heavenly spirits could such perverseness dwell?" (6.788), Milton, through his text, is indeed directing his reader's attention to the line from the *Aeneid* that he is translating—"tantaene animis caelestibus irae?" (1.11); at the same time, the poet is prompting his reader to compare the significance of his line in its context with the significance of Vergil's line in its context. The hermeneutic motion is centrifugal, that is, it leads away from the text of *Paradise Lost*, or, temporally, the motion is retrograde: from Milton back to Vergil. This is the motion of literary tradition, as distinct from literary history. It is at such a moment that the meaning of Milton's text is dependent upon the meaningfulness of the allusive target; it is at such a moment, in other words, that the *responsibility* of the allusive target becomes an issue.

Let us focus our concern more narrowly, then, upon *Paradise Lost*'s literary associations, that is, the notable points of correspondence between a phrase, line, or passage in *Paradise Lost* and a specific phrase, line or passage in another, earlier text— presumably one that Milton is known, or at least likely, to have read. Allusion-mongers would have it that, while Milton's "fit audience" would have caught every oblique echo of Statius and Claudian, we moderns, in our ignorance of the classics, notice little or nothing; this is why we need such guides as Davis Harding and Francis Blessington. But noticing the allusion, interestingly enough, is usually not the problem. Since 1695, when the premier commentary on *Paradise Lost* appeared, a remarkably thorough work by one Patrick Hume, readers eager to catch Milton's many allusions have not had to rely upon the intimacy of their own memories of the Bible, the classics, and the rest of the western cultural tradition through the seventeenth century. Instead, the reader's problem, our problem, has been and remains the interpretation of the resemblances that have been noticed. To be sure, an allusion to Homer, even after it has been pointed out by a commentary, will remain inert if readers have no personal experience of his poetry. But no special privilege is granted to readers simply for being familiar with Homer, Hesiod, Euripides, Plato, Aristotle, Callimachus, Lucretius, Cicero, Catullus, Vergil, Horace, Ovid, Plutarch, Apuleius, and Claudian—to give the roll call of some of Milton's most important classical authorities.

Hume's commentary is an instructive example of the interpretative difficulties inherent in even the best commentaries. He presents the reader with a confusing superabundance of references to the classics. Among these, incidentally, Vergil appears to be cited more often than any other author (roughly eighty citations in book 1 alone), with Ovid running second. Often the mention of Vergil is clearly intended as nothing more than the illustration of some general poetic usage. So states Hume on "Regions of sorrow, doleful shades," at 1.65:

> The dark Regions of the Dead, are, by all the Poets, delineated by Shades: *Ire sub umbras,* is, in Virgil's phrase, to die, *Vitaque cum gemitu fugit indignata sub umbras.* And Hell is so by him described,
>   —Tum Tartarus ipse,
>   Bis patet in praeceps tantum, Tenditque sub
>   umbras. Aen. 6.[2]

That is a lot to say about a commonplace. Only very occasionally does Hume explicitly describe an association that he notes as an "allusion." One of these rare instances is his comment upon *Paradise Lost* 1.328–29, "or with linked thunderbolts / Transfix us," which he links with *Aeneid* 1.44, while throwing in for good measure a mention of Tasso as well:

This [i.e., Milton's line] alludes to the Fate of Ajax Oileus, *Od. E.* imitated by Virg. *Illum expirantem transfixo pectore flammas, Turbine corripuit, scopuloque infixit acuto,* Aen. 1. Who pleaseth to read the Devils Speech to his Damned Assembly in Tasso, Cant. 4. from Stanza 9, *Tartarei Numi di seder piu degni, La soura il Sole,* to Stanza 18, will find our Author has seen him, though borrow'd little of him.

Note the interpretative complexities. The terms *allusion, imitation,* and *borrowing* are used here side by side without any clear distinction. The allusion, says Hume, is to the fate of Ajax Oileus; this suggests a mythological reference. But Hume adduces two textual sources, one of which (the one from Vergil) resembles Milton's line verbally (*transfixo*/"transfix"), though not in great detail. Are we to see in this single word a genuine verbal allusion? In any event, what is the point of the mythological reference? Note that Hume's citation of sources is in error. It is not book 5 (Greek *E*) of the *Odyssey* that contains the account of Ajax's death, but book 4 (lines 499–511). Moreover, the source of the story as Vergil imitates it, here and again elsewhere (*Aeneid* 2.403–4., 6.840), is not the *Odyssey* at all but Euripides' *Troades* 77–78 (see also Ovid, *Metamorphoses* 14.468–69). The differences between Homer's story and that of Euripides are few, but significant enough to determine which tradition Milton would have been following, if he were actually alluding to anyone here, which I doubt. (In Homer, Poseidon overwhelms Ajax's ship. In Euripides, Vergil, and Ovid, Athene sinks it with a thunderbolt and then transfixes Ajax on a cliff.)

I mention Hume's misdirection here not in order to disparage him. His errors seem often the consequence of quoting from what must have been, by our standards today, a prodigious memory. Even if his self-reliance does not recommend

the scrupulousness of his scholarly methods, it is worth taking
note of, for Hume, if anyone, must have been a "fit audience" for Milton's poetry. Hume's offhand recollection of the
passage suggests that it is not impossible to read the classics
and *Paradise Lost* together; we need only to understand that
interpretation takes place in the memory. Moreover, Hume's
venial mistakes suggest the difference between the interpretative experience when we rely upon a commentary, on the
one hand, and when, on the other hand, we enjoy a more
intimate acquaintance with the models of Milton's poem.[3] We
are not usually supposed to respond to an allusion by thinking of precise book and line numbers, that is, by whispering
to ourselves, "Aha! *Odyssey* 5," or "Hmm . . . *Troades* 77–78?"
Even if we set *Paradise Lost* aside momentarily to check the
passage referred to in the notes, we will not be able to judge
its significance simply by comparing the line or two cited as
the direct source. We must first of all respond to the allusion
emotionally. I confess I do not like the word *emotional,* but a
better one does not occur to me, and it is important to keep in
mind that an allusion has an affective dimension whose importance is hard to exaggerate, but almost impossible to discuss
critically in any detail. Second, the source or target must be
understood in context. The citation in the note, then, is at best
a reminder of something you already know fairly well or, at
least, a recommendation for future study.

Let me conclude this excursus on Hume's commentary by
observing that sometimes allusions that are critically important are noticed without any comment upon their point, as at
1.84, "But O how fallen! how changed!" where Hume simply
quotes *Aeneid* 2.274–75, "quantum mutatus ab illo." There
it is: Hume has fingered the allusion. But we must still ask
ourselves what can be made of it. Some of the problems con-

fronting the reader of Hume are absent from the better-orga-
nized and more copious commentaries of Newton and Todd,
as well as more recent commentaries. But the fundamental
questions—how important an association is, and what kind of
significance it has—were not answered by them, and persist
not only in the best modern commentaries (where the relative scarcity of classical citations suggests greater selectiveness
without proving it), but also in criticism concerning the topic.[4]

Lesser Forms of Literary Intertextuality

The analysis that follows is necessarily brief and suggestive
rather than dialectically thorough. It attempts to answer two
questions. First, can the various critical terms in use (such
as *borrowing* and *allusion*) be usefully distinguished, in regard
either to denotation or connotation? And second, do these
terms in any way correspond to whatever different kinds of
critical consequence may be observed among the verbal connections between *Paradise Lost* and its predecessors, especially
the *Aeneid*? I submit that both questions should be answered
affirmatively.[5]

Of least interpretative consequence is that link between
texts which consists of the mere *appropriation* of a word, line,
or passage from a source without regard for its context there,
or at least without any intent that the appropriation should
call the source to the reader's mind. True, comparison of an
appropriation with its source may illuminate aspects of the
poet's compositional technique. But the appropriation cannot
be called an allusion nor even a reference, since both terms
connote that the reader's attention is being directed *back* to
the source. When Milton makes Belial speak of God's "red
right hand" (2.174), he may or may not have been consciously
recalling Horace's "rubente dextera" (*Odes* 1.2.3–4). Commen-

tators have noted the similarity between the phrases, but the discriminating reader will ask, here as always, what the meaning of the connection might be. We have no reason to suppose that the phrase was peculiarly meaningful to Milton. I will argue later that he does take very profound account of one of Horace's odes, but it is not *Odes* 1.2. Nor does the phrase stand out as one of the jewels of Milton's emulation of the ancients. He does not rework the phrase in any way that might demonstrate his poetic inventiveness or justify a boast of poetic improvement upon his predecessors.[6] The best one can say is that the phrase is striking: it struck Milton, and he took it. My guess is that he did not think of Horace as he wrote it. Of course, it is almost impossible to demonstrate that a suspected intertextual link is merely an appropriation, but one should always keep the possibility in mind.

Much more important are those intertextual links that may be designated *references*, since the poet means for us to recognize them.

The first of these references is the general *reminiscence* of a previous author's style, technique, or language, without necessary reference to a specific source passage. Every poet of secondary epic has been to some extent influenced by Homeric style. (This, of course, is not to be confused with the oral-formulaic style, as described by Milman Parry and Albert Lord.) Major aspects of Milton's style throughout *Paradise Lost*, such as the inversions of his syntax, the elaboration of his periods, and his use of unrhymed verse, are strongly reminiscent of a conglomerate classical epic style. Particularly when he deals at length with Satan and his followers, Milton's classicism is highlighted by the more frequent use of elaborate similes, geographical and mythological names, and, of course, references to classical literature. Concerning what Davis Harding calls "the Homeric ring" of *Paradise Lost* 6, Newton wrote, "One may plainly see that he has read him [i.e., Homer], even where he does not imitate him."[7] When truly epic action is represented in epic diction, the diction tends to seem inevitable. But the significance of this diction as a reference to antiquity is unmistakable in the clearer example of mock epic or ancient satire (as in Horace's hexameter *saturae*), where the style is isolated from the context. Reminiscence need not be general. Local reminiscences of Spenser, Shakespeare, and the Bible are found in *Paradise Lost*, and in the work of other authors whose styles are more flexible than Milton's (Horace or Petronius in antiquity, Joyce or Pound in this century), reminiscence may be a most important poetic resource. Interpreters of Milton have to keep the possibility of reminiscence in mind because it tends to muddy the waters, sometimes making the identification of more precise textual references rather difficult.

A second reference is the *echo* of a specific line or passage that enhances the later poem, but that does not involve a deeply or precisely significant relation between the meaning of the source in its context and the meaning of the present passage in its context. This kind of echo is very close to reminiscence as I just described it, and in practice the distinction may frequently be imperceptible, but the echo's evocation of a specific source is significant, albeit in an indefinable or imprecise way. Unfortunately, it is echo above all, I think, that we moderns are likely to miss when we read Milton. The critical allusion, my preoccupation in the next two chapters, will be shown to be almost philosophical in its operation; but the echo is profoundly poetic. John Hollander, in a fine study of this trope, describes echo as "a way of alluding that is inherently poetic, rather than expository, and that makes new metaphor rather than learned gestures."[8] Echo is a kind of resonance; Hollander is particularly interested in its aural qualities. I am more concerned with the qualities of echo that cause it to be confused with allusion so frequently.

Often an echo carries emotional undertones. Vergil likens the dying Euryalus to a fallen flower:

> purpureus ueluti cum flos succisus aratro
> languescit moriens, lassoue papauera collo
> demisere caput pluuia cum forte grauantur.
>
> (*Aeneid* 9.435–37)

> (just as when the ruddy flower nipped by the plow's
> edge droops, dying, or as the weary-necked poppies
> drop their heads when a chance rain-shower weighs
> upon them.)

The Homeric source is a simile applied to the otherwise insignificant Gorgythion:

> μήκων δ᾽ ὡς ἑτέρωσε κάρη βάλεν, ἥ τ᾽ ἐνὶ κήπῳ,
> καρπῷ βριθομένη νοτίησί τε εἰαρινῇσιν,
> ὣς ἑτέρωσ᾽ ἤμυσε κάρη πήληκι βαρυνθέν.
>
> (*Iliad* 8.306–8)

> (as when a poppy in the garden drops its head to one
> side, weighed down with its fruit or with the spring rain,
> so his head fell to one side under the helmet's burden.)

The martial contexts of the two passages are similar, and this reference to Homer may be better described as a weak allusion (see below) than as an echo. But the passage from Homer is not the only source or even the most important source here. The simile possesses a distinct emotional resonance for the

reader who recalls the simile in Catullus 11 of a flower cut by
the plow:

> nec meum respectet, ut ante, amorem,
> qui illius culpa cecidit uelut prati
> ultimi flos, praetereunte postquam
>   tactus aratro est.
>
>   (Catullus 11.21–24)[9]

> (and let her [Lesbia] not look to my love as before; it has
> fallen by her fault like a flower at the far edge of a field,
> after having been grazed by a passing plow.)

Vergil's lines do not *refer* to Catullus' lines. Vergil's lines resonate with the pathos of Catullus' simile, but do not draw attention to its fuller significance in the context of the entire poem,
because the amatory (and somewhat indelicate) connotations
of the simile in Catullus' poem would be wholly inappropriate in the quite dissimilar context of Euryalus' death. Gian
Biagio Conte finds a very similar echo of Catullus in *Aeneid* 6.
Aeneas' statement to Dido, "inuitus, o regina, tuo de litore
cessi" (*Aeneid* 6.460: "Unwillingly, o queen, did I depart from
your shore"), has its source in Catullus' "inuita, o regina, tuo
de uertice cessi" (66.39: "Unwillingly, o queen, did I depart
from your head"). The line in Catullus, of course, concerns
a lock of hair—is actually spoken by a lock of hair—and is
distinctly mock-heroic. Conte's explanation is that the lines
in Catullus employ a genuinely pathetic style (Conte uses the
term *register* here), which is deliberately misapplied to express
a comic content. When Vergil reuses the line, he expects the
reader to shear off the inappropriate content and concentrate
on the register or style. Vergil does this to compliment Catullus
and at the same time to outdo him.[10]

On a larger scale, the encounter between Aeneas and Dido

in the underworld (*Aeneid* 6.450–51.) echoes the encounter
between Odysseus and the shade of Ajax (*Odyssey* 11.543–
44.). The Aeneas–Dido scene does not imply or depend upon
a specific interpretation of the scene between Odysseus and
Ajax. There are certain significant contrasts, particularly that
Aeneas pleads at some length with Dido and is clearly pained
at her rebuff, while Odysseus, though he expresses his regret
for Ajax's sorrow, wastes no time on Ajax once it is clear that he
is not going to speak. But Vergil's reworking of the scene falls
short of suggesting a parallel between Odysseus' relationship
with Ajax and Aeneas' relationship with Dido, or between any
other aspect of the contexts of the two scenes. The significance
of the reworking consists in two things: it draws attention to
itself as a facet of Vergil's emulation of Homer; and, specifically, it amplifies an echo of the scene's pathos in Homer into
a high pitch of emotion.[11]

It is relative indifference to context, then, that distinguishes
the echo. A *borrowing*, on the other hand, is almost an allusion, in that the contexts of the later passage and its target are
analogous. The link between a borrowing and its source may
be very weak, but borrowing is distinguished, at least in theory,
from mere appropriation by the fact that it is more than an
aspect of the poet's compositional technique. The following
passage contains several Biblical borrowings:

> Mean while the eternal eye, whose sight discerns
> Abstrusest thoughts, from forth his holy mount
> And from within the golden lamps that burn
> Nightly before him, saw without their light
> Rebellion rising, saw in whom, how spread
> Among the sons of morn, what multitudes
> Were banded to oppose his high decree.
>
> (5.711–17)

If we disregard the more complicated references of "the eternal eye" and "holy mount," this passage borrows from St. John's description, "Before the throne burn seven torches of fire, which are the seven spirits of God" (Revelation 4.5, with which compare Zechariah 4.2), and Isaiah's verse, "How you are fallen from heaven, O Day Star, son of Dawn!" (Isaiah 14.12). The contextual correspondence between these passages is, of course, a matter of the interpretation of the Biblical passages, and in Milton's time interpreters claimed a lot of latitude. Basil Willey's remark is to the point:

> To the modern mind it is, of course, just the complete absence of all historical sense that is so remarkable in early biblical criticism. The whole of Scripture is treated as homogeneous, and any passage can be connected with any other for the extraction of further meanings.[12]

This fact makes it extremely difficult to interpret Milton's Biblical references, which are at the same time more abundant and individually less significant than his classical references. (In regard to the instant case, it may suffice to point out that Isaiah 14.12 is one of the major Biblical texts relevant to the character of Satan.) At the same time, it may be that Milton's allusions to the Bible are exemplary, because they indicate so clearly the necessity of interpreting the target as well as the text that alludes to it.

The presence or absence of contextual correspondence is more readily discernible in the case of Milton's classical borrowings, and therefore the difference between an echo and a borrowing can be determined more confidently. These lines from book 1 describe Satan:

> He now prepared
> To speak; whereat their doubled ranks they bend

From wing to wing, and half enclose him round
With all his peers: attention held them mute.
                    (1.615–18)

We have here only an echo of the opening words of the second book of the *Aeneid*, "conticuere omnes, intentique ora
tenebant" ("They all fell silent and kept their eyes on him at-
tentively").[13] There is no elaborate correspondence between
Satan's address to the fallen angels and Aeneas' two-book narrative to the Carthaginians. Structurally, Aeneas' retrospective
tale corresponds more closely to the tale Raphael tells Adam
and Eve. Yet the correspondence between the English and
Latin phrases was noted by Hume and has been commented
on repeatedly since. Its significance is, I think, connotative.

Another, and more interesting, example of echo as distinct
from borrowing is found at the end of the angelic hymn in
book 3.

Hail, Son of God, saviour of men, thy name
Shall be the copious matter of my song
Henceforth, and never shall my harp thy praise
Forget, nor from thy Father's praise disjoin.
                    (3.412–15)

One commentator (Alistair Fowler) has cited the close of the
hymn to Hercules in *Aeneid* 8 as the source of Milton's lines:

salue, uera Iouis proles, decus addite diuis,
et nos et tua dexter adi pede sacra secundo.
                    (8.301–2)

(Hail, true offspring of Jupiter, a glory added to the
gods! Come graciously, with lucky step, to us and to
your rites.)

But Vergil himself is drawing upon the formulaic close of nearly all the Homeric hymns. He may have been borrowing consciously from the conclusion of the brief hymn to Heracles, "Hail, lord, son of Zeus! Grant me reputation [ἀρετήν] and prosperity." The conclusion of the hymn to Delian Apollo is more apposite to the passage in Milton: "I shall never cease to praise far-darting Apollo of the silver bow, whom fair-haired Leto bore." In this instance in Milton, a rather pronounced echo comes daringly close to allusion, but is restrained by the demands of decorum and by the relative obscurity of the source. (Hume does not note the connection, and later editors before Fowler by and large missed it as well. Hughes says nothing.) This is a closet tour de force of Milton's classicism and must remain so, for an open allusion here would be indecorous in the extreme.

A few examples of borrowing should suffice to characterize this reference. The description of how Satan, "extended long and large / Lay floating many a rood" (1.195–96) borrows from Vergil's description of the nine *iugera* over which Tityos sprawls (*Aeneid* 6.596).[14] Milton's "Titanian, or Earth-born" (1.198) borrows from Vergil's "genus antiquum Terrae, Titania pubes" (*Aeneid* 6.580: "the ancient race of Earth, Titanian offspring"). The words "a sylvan scene" (4.140), with which Milton describes Paradise, are taken from Vergil's description of the place on the shores of Africa where Aeneas and his followers land, "syluis scaena coruscis" (1.164: "a scene of shimmering groves").[15] A borrowing is not necessarily more meaningful than an echo. It does contribute a little to the reader's sense of the immenseness of Milton's learning, and this sense is not without rhetorical consequence. Like a scholar's notes, Milton's innumerable borrowings, if recognized, are the proofs of his authority. But if intertextual reference were nothing more than evidence of the author's erudition, it would be a self-defeating game, since the most impressive reference would be the one so arcane that nobody caught it. More useful is the hypothesis that even the most trivial references contribute to Milton's grand allusion to antiquity. But this hypothesis merely notes that echo and borrowing both contribute to a broad, general strategy. Their significance is cumulative, not particular, and as Robert M. Adams observes acutely, an accumulation of weak links does not lend any one of them greater strength.[16]

It must be admitted that there is something inherently uninteresting, or even suspicious, about borrowing. Do a poet's borrowings constitute an acknowledgment of his debt to the literary tradition, or are they evidence of lack of creative power? This uncertainty is not new. Vergil's detractors wrote books cataloging his *furta* ("thefts"). Vergil's defense is famous: "facilius esse Herculi clauam quam Homero uersum subripere" (*Vita Donati* 46: "It is easier to take Hercules' club away from him than to take a verse from Homer").[17] This statement calls to mind the remarks of another poet who has been accused of plagiarism, T. S. Eliot, in his essay on Philip Massinger:

> Immature poets imitate: mature poets steal; bad poets deface what they take, and good poets make it into something better, or at least something different. The good poet welds his theft into a whole of feeling which is unique, utterly different from that from which it was torn; the bad poet throws it into something which has no cohesion. A good poet will usually borrow from authors remote in time, or alien in language, or diverse in interest.[18]

Eliot speaks somewhat loosely in the last sentence of "borrowing," but his choice of the descriptive term "theft" must rule out the use of the term "borrowing": you cannot borrow and steal a thing at the same time. Whether the poet's theft was conscious or unconscious, as must often be the case, is no matter. What I am calling borrowing, then, corresponds to what Eliot (to judge from his first sentence) would call imitation. It is, according to Eliot, a mark of *immaturity*. The very notion of borrowing, then, implies a kind of weakness, or need in the poet. And yet Vergil, whom Eliot in another essay (the notorious "What Is a Classic?") found to be Europe's most *mature* poet, acknowledges himself to be a desperate debtor. I would claim that borrowing contributes in an important way to the allusive strategy of secondary epic such as Milton's. But borrowing is redeemed only if it is accompanied by what I will call the strong or *critical* allusion.

In the essay on Massinger, Eliot's main concern is with a dramatic poetry that is not allusive at all in the manner of *Paradise Lost*. Accordingly he is indifferent to the interpretative dimension of the relationship between a great poet and his great predecessors and is instead intent upon the craft of allusive poetry as viewed from the poet's or playwright's own perspective. Nevertheless, his statement suggests that the victim of the great poet's theft is usually a lesser poet or not a poet at all. Seneca, Plutarch, and Ovid were among Shakespeare's victims; Eliot also mentions Montaigne in a sentence immediately following the passage just quoted. Now, the poet of secondary epic is not above purloining a line or even a scene whenever he can. Apollonius and Ennius are among Vergil's victims; Du Bartas and Spenser are among those of Milton. But unlike the dramatist, whose interests ordinarily lie elsewhere than in allusion to the past, the poet of secondary epic primarily sets himself against not a lesser but a greater poet, one who will vigorously resist attack. And he aims not to snatch an occasional verse, but to rework the entire genre. The critical allusion is the weapon that he uses.

The Critical Allusion

The word *allusion* itself is worth examining. Its verbal form, *allude,* derives from Latin *adludo* "make a joke," and, especially, "play on words." Thus when Iulus unwittingly fulfills the prophecy of Celaeno the harpy (see 3.250–51) by remarking that they are "eating their tables"—he refers to the tortilla-like cakes on which they had placed their food—Vergil rounds off the quotation with the words, "inquit Iulus, / nec plura, adludens" (*Aeneid* 7.116–17: "thus spoke Iulus and no more, playing on words"). In later Latin the word came to mean "suggest" or "refer to obliquely," its proper meanings in English today. In contrast to the terms *influence* and *debt, allusion* affirms the poet's free intention to enter into the relationship with his predecessor. In contrast to *source* and *background,* two other common critical terms whose connotations are often overlooked, *allusion* suggests a retrograde motion originating in the later text and directing the reader back to the former text, the target. Allusion then is not really a by-product of the poem's creation, the dimension, described above, in which Eliot was interested; it designates, rather, a relationship that is an intended aspect of the poem as an *interpretandum,* a "thing to be interpreted." Allusion, in other words, is neither borrowing nor theft. The study of it does not involve piercing through the text in order to uncover what lies behind it. It involves, rather, the recognition of what the surface of the text is doing. Finally, in contrast to the term *use*—critics often speak of Milton's "use of the classics"—the element of play in allusion suggests a more amiable, more polite, more civilized relationship, a rivalry perhaps, but one that has achieved equilibrium. *Playing against* suggests neither use nor conquest.

At every claimed point of association between two texts, critics should ask, What is the meaning of this? I would propose, as a rule of thumb, that if a point of association seems to serve as the locus for a much wider complex of significant correspondences between the texts, then it may be an allusion. But it is precisely because the true allusion initiates such a variety of comparisons that, if the author is to avoid appearing purely imitative, it must contain an element of contrast as well as comparison. This is what I call the *critical allusion*. My use of the word *critical* is deliberately ambiguous: I mean by it to suggest both that the allusion contains a criticism of its target and that the allusion possesses extraordinary hermeneutic importance. As it is used by great poets at least, the critical allusion inevitably has a double operation: it associates the passage and its target in a strong and normally rather obvious manner, and simultaneously it prevents the association from being total—often to the point of allowing the association to develop into direct conflict. Frequently the allusive text distinguishes itself from its target at least in part by means of verbal caricature or parody, a kind of subtextual mockery of the target that deliberate provokes—or should provoke—an attentive reader to object.

Most often the contrast is a matter of reworking the source in some way so as to alter or (as frequently is the case) reverse its significance. Since we shall presently be dealing at length with Milton's critical allusions to Horace, Hesiod, and Vergil, I offer here two examples of Vergil's allusions to Homer. The targets of both are located within a few lines of one another near the end of the *Iliad*.

As in a dream a man cannot overtake the one who flees him—the one cannot escape nor the other overtake him—just so, Achilles could not catch Hector on foot, nor could

Hector slip away. How could Hector escape the spirits of death, if Apollo were not standing near by him this one last time, stirring up his courage and his nimble knees? But god-like Achilles shook his head at his people, for them not to cast their bitter spears at Hector, lest the thrower snatch the glory and Achilles himself be second. (*Iliad* 22.199–207)

The dream simile, used in Homer to illustrate the eerie inconclusiveness of Achilles' pursuit of Hector, is applied in *Aeneid* 12 to Turnus alone and elaborated so that it becomes (as is Vergil's wont) not an illustration of Turnus' physical inability to outrun Aeneas, but an image of the paralyzing terror which has gripped his soul:

> ac uelut in somnis, oculos ubi languida pressit
> nocte quies, nequiquam auidos extendere cursus
> uelle uidemur et in mediis conatibus aegri
> succidimus; non lingua ualet, non corpore notae
> sufficiunt uires nec uox aut uerba sequuntur.
>
> (12.908–12)

> (as in a dream, when at night dull rest weighs upon our eyes, and we see ourselves trying to run ahead, eagerly but in vain, and in the midst of our efforts we fall down exhausted; the tongue is worthless, the ordinary strength of our body is inadequate, and neither sound nor words come out.

This, the final simile of the *Aeneid* is an emblem of Vergil's major reworking of Homer, the internalization of the action. Homer draws on dream-experience to describe what is ultimately for him a footrace, at which he is the spectator. Vergil not only dwells on the dream experience itself more fully, but actually injects himself into it; hence the first-person verbs (*uidemur, succidimus*).

Just after the dream simile in *Iliad* 22, Achilles shakes his head at his own comrades lest someone kill Hector first and rob the Achaean hero of his glory (lines 205–7). At *Aeneid* 12.760–62, the situation is similar, but its meaning is completely reversed. Turnus, as he runs from Aeneas, calls to his comrades for help, but Aeneas forbids anyone to offer it:

> Aeneas mortem contra praesensque minatur
> exitium, si quisquam adeat, terretque trementis
> excisurum urbem minitans et saucius instat.
>
> (12.760–62)

> (Aeneas in turn threatens death and immediate destruction to anyone who approaches, and he terrifies them, threatening to demolish their city, while they quake and he, although wounded, presses on.

Aeneas does not forbid his comrades to kill his foe, as Achilles had done: he forbids Turnus' comrades to help him. He has no concern here for personal glory—only for the consummation of this individual combat, the alternative to general war, which had earlier been agreed to by Turnus, but which was delayed when an anonymous Rutulian wounded Aeneas (12.319–20).

Allusion as Enthymeme

The interpretation of allusions presents a particular practical challenge to recent hermeneutics. The notion of authorial intentionality seems suspiciously vague when considered in general terms, yet it is such an essential part of the ordinary understanding of any particular allusion that the author expected the best readers to recognize it. We do not say that

Milton alludes to the Romantics that followed him, and we do not allow that any resemblance between Milton's poem and any earlier literature may be counted as an allusion, however unlikely it is that Milton was familiar with the passage. Gian Biagio Conte notes that we used to think of the author as expecting readers to have a certain competence, but he thinks that it is better now to say that the author, through the text, "*establishes* the competence of his Model Reader, that is, the author constructs the addressee and motivates the text in order to do so." As a consequence,

> the limit implicit in the notion of the literary genre as a "horizon of expectations" may have become outdated. Although this notion has been heuristically extremely fertile, it does, in the final analysis, appear static, impeding the image of the text as process.[19]

I think it is quite valuable to abandon the idea of allusion as a sort of inside joke; I will attempt in the following chapters of this book to demonstrate that Milton's major allusions are part of the design of the work. However, I cannot deny that this design is profoundly rhetorical, and not rhetorical in the modern philosophical sense, the sense of the title of Conte's book, *The Rhetoric of Imitation*, but rhetorical in the classical sense.

Aristotle in the *Rhetoric* (1.2 and 2.22) notes that deductive reasoning in rhetorical contexts proceeds by means of implied syllogisms called *enthymemes*. Defining this term historically is not an easy task because it was used in various ways, but it may not be an oversimplification to define enthymeme for our purposes as a syllogism with one or more of its premises implied rather than stated.[20] Syllogisms take the following form:

> *major premise*: All men are mortal.
> *minor premise*: Socrates is a man.
> *conclusion*: Socrates is mortal.

An enthymeme, in its pure form, would omit either the major or the minor premise, thus: All men are mortal, therefore Socrates is mortal [minor premise omitted]; or, Socrates is a man, therefore he is mortal [major premise omitted]. Aristotle notes that ordinary men are often more effective speakers than the uncommonly learned. The latter are inclined to employ lengthy chains of deductions in which syllogicm is linked to syllogism, but listeners, unless they are themselves learned, find such argumentation tedious and therefore unpersuasive. The ordinary man, on the other hand, leaves his general premises unstated. He argues by reference to notions close at hand. Aristotle's remarks on the enthymeme are tantalizingly limited. Quintilian says more about the subject, and focuses especially on the use of enthymemes in refutation, which seems especially appropriate to our present concerns.[21] Quintilian's treatment is highly technical and at times difficult to follow, but it is apparent that the enthymeme's effectiveness as a rhetorical tool is more than a matter of efficiency, that is, the fact that it is less cumbersome type of argumentation is not the only reason to use it.

It seems to me that the enthymeme has two somewhat different, almost contrary, effects. Most obviously, it tacitly prompts the auditor to cooperate with the orator by referring to an understanding or belief that the orator expects the auditor to share. So Quintilian (5.14.1) quotes an enthymeme from Cicero's *Pro Ligario* 6.19 in which the orator comments on the succcess of Caesar in the civil wars: "At that point the issue was uncertain, since there was something to be approved on either side. But now we must judge as superior that side in the controversy which even the gods supported." Omitted here is the notion that the gods could only support the better cause. But there is more to this example than that: Cicero omits as well the proposition that the success of Caesar is evidence of the

gods' support. It may be that he employs enthymeme to bury
the second premise, or it may even be that he wishes to cast
upon it an ironic shadow, visible only to those who are paying
attention.[22] With this example in mind, it is perhaps not difficult to see how the enthymeme can also be used as a kind
of rhetorical trick, allowing the orator to finesse a point by
omitting it as one of the premises. Horace in the *Ars Poetica*,
expatiating on his favorite theme, prosody, says, "Not every
judge can recognize verses that are unmusical, and Roman
poets have been undeservedly indulged in the past" (263–64).
We have here a major premise and a conclusion; the omitted
minor premise is the many or most of the works of the older
Roman masters were in fact not up to Horace's standards (a
claim he makes more explicitly in the epistle to Augustus).
Horace does not, in fact, expect his audience—the Pisos—to
believe this themselves already; on the contrary, because he
suspects that they may resist this statement if it is made directly, he tucks it in between two other statements, where the
reader inevitably, almost unconsciously, supplies it. Thus the
ingenuous reader supposes that he or she has come up with
the idea.

   This, I submit, is quite similar to the way that true allusion
works—and the witty con worked by Horace in the lines just
cited does, in fact, quite closely resemble the clever attacks on
the ancients that Milton makes in some of his most important
allusions. Allusion is *enthymemic*: the poet tacitly prompts the
reader to supply a term that is left unstated. The notion of
true allusion as enthymemic does not compromise the idea of
literature as *process*, as Conte fears, because, as I have understood it, the critical allusion enjoins the reader to engage in
the interpretation of the earlier work, the target of the allusion, as well as of the later work, where the allusion originates.
It is not the notion of a "horizon of expectations" that is out-

moded and static, but the way Conte understands allusion in the context of such a notion. It follows from my understanding of it that allusion is not a matter of stylistic elegance, not an enhancement of the esthetic dimension of the work, but an indispensable mechanism of its argumentation. In the next few chapters I will show what happens when the reader declines to cooperate with the poet unthinkingly, that is, when he or she declines to be Milton's dupe.

How important, then, are these various intertextual links between Milton's poem and the classical texts? This is a controverted matter. One fine scholar claims the "Vergil's almost constant use of Homer . . . always involves allusion," but this is surely wrong.[23] Even allowing for the fact that this scholar was not using *allusion* precisely as I have described the term here, and allowing further for the difference between the cases of Milton and Vergil, it is nevertheless true that a good many of the verbal references to major pre-texts in both Milton and Vergil are matters of relatively minor import.[24] Still, one can go too far in the other direction as well. Another fine classical scholar, in a thorough and authoritative introductory book on the *Aeneid*, wrote that the Homeric echoes in the *Aeneid*

> only *rarely* enhance the significance of the Virgilian context in which they appear; and for this reason the reader unacquainted with the Homeric poems will not be at any *essential* disadvantage.   [emphasis added][25]

But this is a non sequitur: a rare disadvantage might nonetheless be an "essential" one. I maintain, against the prior trend of criticism at least in this century, that out of the welter of Milton's references to the classics, only a handful deserve to be called allusions. But I will try to demonstrate in the chapters that follow that the importance of this handful would be hard

to exaggerate, and that a reader who is not on fairly intimate
terms with the targets of the allusions is very likely to miss
something "essential."

Of course, this last scholar is writing an introduction to the
Aeneid, and he wishes not to discourage his readers, who are
more likely to be young students than other scholars. But this
sort of misrepresentation, however tactful, will in the end only
confuse. That readers unacquainted with the Homeric poems
might greatly enjoy reading the *Aeneid* and might even derive
profound benefit from their study of the poem need not be
denied. It need not even be denied that some of these readers
might go on to find useful things to say about the poem. However, if they are at all searching, will they not soon suspect that
an entire dimension of the poem is merely hinted at—not just
one of many equally important dimensions, but the one out of
which all the others arise?

As a rhetorical figure, allusion is *ab origine* profoundly historical; an allusive relationship is initiated by a verbal gesture
of the later poet. I conclude by noting that this is not to say that
the meaning of an allusion is accessible only from the modern
side of the bridge. In fact, as I suggested above in regard to
Hume's commentary, the interpreter of allusions deals with all
of the texts in the arena of memory, where everything exists in
a sort of simultaneity. Once the allusive relationship has been
established, the earlier locus has been provided with a new,
enriching context that those readers who are aware of it may
not wish to ignore. The original Museum of Fine Arts in Houston, William Ward Watkin's limestone temple of high culture
with its majestic Ionic columns (1924, 1926), was permanently
placed in a new context by the later additions designed by
Mies van der Rohe (1958, 1974). You can walk around outside and regard the old facade in isolation; from the right

perspective the modernist additions in the "back" are not obtrusively visible. But the building that you view in this manner no longer has any meaning in itself—if I can use the word *meaning* to denote the experience of using a building—for you can no longer enter the museum through Watkin's front gates, which have been sealed. The old building now is accessible only through the new, and this makes an incalculable difference. *Paradise Lost,* I would maintain, is the grand foyer of the classical tradition in English. To walk through Milton's edifice and try not to notice it is folly; to refuse to enter through Milton's doors at all is in some way to resign oneself to looking at the old books from the outside, on what has now become the back lawn.

2

Descende caelo:
Thought

ἀγαθὴ δ' Ἔρις ἥδε βροτοῖσιν.

καὶ κεραμεὺς κεραμεῖ κοτέει καὶ τέκτονι τέκτων,

καὶ πτωχὸς πτωχῷ φθονέει καὶ ἀοιδὸς ἀοιδῷ.*

—Hesiod, *Works and Days*

Milton is widely understood to have urged a "critique" of the classics in *Paradise Lost.*[1] The primary evidence is abundant and well known to Miltonists, but not so unequivocal as some have thought. The critique inferred by certain critics from Milton's text usually boils down to the revelation that Homer, Vergil, and the other champions of Greco-Roman poetry were pagans. For example, referring to the sort of demonic typology that constituted the classical hermeneutics of certain church fathers, Philip J. Gallagher contends that "Milton believed" that the myth of divine succession in Hesiod's *Theogony* was a lie inspired by Satan, and that the Hesiodic details in *Paradise Lost* 6 are designed to expose the titanomachy as a fraud.[2]

*"This Strife is good for mortals. Potter envies potter and carpenter envies carpenter; one beggar is jealous of another, and poet resents poet."

43

How seriously can we take this sort of thing? Presumably the critics who have expounded the critique theory feel as literary historians that it would be anachronistic to fault Milton with being a man of his time—though they tolerate Milton's faulting Homer and Vergil for the same reason. But the studies to which I am referring are, in fact, more tendentious than that. Invariably, Milton, explicitly or implicitly, is praised at the expense of the classics. This is not fair, but criticism, I suppose, is always tempted to aggrandize its object. Nevertheless, there is a most un-Miltonic irony here. Milton is praised for doing the very thing—namely, exercising his judgment—that the critics would prefer at least to *seem* not to being doing themselves.

On the other hand, it would be equally thoughtless to deny that Milton is somehow challenging—perhaps I should say taunting—the classics. That challenge, or that taunt, is not made in his critical writing in prose, but rather is insinuated into the design and argument of his epic. In this way, I submit, it escapes its origin in the parochial controversies of the seventeenth century, along with the poetry that conveys it, and becomes a matter of enduring interest. What is that challenge and why has it remained unanswered? Is it unanswerable?

"Above the Aonian Mount"

In Milton's avowal that his poem "with no middle flight intends to soar / Above the Aonian mount" (*Paradise Lost* 1.14–15), most readers have seen only a general ambition to surpass the classical epics.[3] Vergil, in the *Georgics,* expresses his ambition similarly:

> primus ego in patriam mecum, modo uita supersit,
> Aonio rediens deducam uertice Musas.
>
> (3.10–11)

(If only I live long enough, I will be the first to return
from the Aonian mountain top, leading the Muses into
my native land.)

Though these lines occur in the most Hesiodic of Roman
poems, it is clear that Vergil is not thinking of Hesiod here.
The ambition expressed has not been fulfilled by the writing
of the *Georgics,* but instead looks forward to the writing of the
Aeneid.[4] The numerous later references in antiquity and the
Renaissance to the Aonian mount, alias Helicon,[5] are no more
pointed. Nevertheless, there is embedded here a particular
reference to Hesiod's *Theogony.* By "embedded," I mean to suggest that the significance of the reference is not immediately
apparent and takes time to develop.

Helicon is not simply a place dear to the Muses, like Par-
nassus, nor simply where the inspirational springs Aganippe
or Hippocrene are to be found. It is specifically the scene of
the greatest theophany of the Muses in classical literature, that
which Hesiod presents at the opening of the *Theogony.* It thus
corresponds to the Biblical mountains that Milton names in
the same context, which were sites of divine inspirations in the
Bible. It is worth noting that the association of the Muses with
Helicon does not occur in Homer.[6] Though the Heliconian
cult of the Muses may have antedated Hesiod, it was he who
transmitted to later literary tradition their primary association
with this locale.

If it seems inherently implausible that Milton should elect
as a champion of classical poetry a figure generally regarded
today by nonclassicists (and even sometimes by classicists) as
minor, let me say again that this election is covert. Of course,
as one of the two earliest extant Greek poets, he would not
have seemed so minor to the well-educated man of Milton's

day. Thamyris was only a name and Orpheus not much more, while Musaeus was by Milton's college days no longer taken as the most ancient poet. But there are several weightier reasons why Milton's use of Hesiod here can be seen as inevitable and right.

Milton will have followed Renaissance critical consensus in judging Hesiod to be slightly later than Homer; but Hesiod was the undeniable classical prototype of the divinely inspired poet. One finds in the Homeric epics no precedent for the expansive and yet deeply intimate confessions that Milton felt his own invocations had to be. Homer's invocations are brief (seldom longer than three lines) and impersonal; they serve chiefly to punctuate the narratives that surround them.[7] (In these respects Vergil differs little from Homer.) Hesiod, on the other hand, describes at length how the Muses came to him on Mount Helicon, gave him a laurel staff, and breathed into him so that he might sing of "things that will be and things that have been before" (*Theogony* 32). After vividly describing his own poetic commissioning (22–34), Hesiod proceeds to narrate the birth of the Muses and to describe their collective character and concerns in what amounts to an extended meditation on the nature of poetry (36–103); finally he invokes their aid for the singing of the rest of the *Theogony*. This is virtually the only extended passage in classical poetry of which the Muses are the principal subject.[8]

Moreover, Hesiod resembles in uncanny ways both his Biblical counterpart, Moses, and his modern rival, Milton himself. Milton refers to Moses as

> That shepherd, who first taught the chosen seed,
> In the beginning how the heavens and earth
> Rose out of chaos.   (1.8–10)

The characterization of Moses as a shepherd was uncommon, but we who have never seen a real shepherd should not jump to find a metaphor here. Milton directs the reader specifically to the third chapter of Exodus, where God presents himself to Moses, who has been out on Mount Sinai pasturing the flock of his father-in-law. One context calls up another: Hesiod, too, had been pasturing sheep on a hillside when the Muses called him (*Theogony* 23).[9] Furthermore, the next two lines in Milton's proem are more literally referable to Hesiod than to Moses. The Muses tell Hesiod "from the beginning" (ἐξ ἀρχῆς, *Theogony* 115) "how the heaven and the earth and all things else rose out of chaos." "Chaos" (χάος) is Hesiod's own word, first attested in Greek here in the *Theogony* (line 116).

Hesiod's affinities with Milton are broader but equally strong. More than almost any other ancient poet, Hesiod purposes "to justify the ways of God to men." Justice (δίκη), both human and divine, is the foremost theme of the *Works and Days,* a poem purportedly provoked by a bad verdict at court. The deteriorative account of human history promoted by Hesiod in the myths of Pandora and of the five ages probably did not directly influence Milton, but it clearly resonates in his account of the sin of Eve and the decline of human civilization consequent upon the Fall. The *Theogony,* on the other hand, whose overriding aim I take to be the "justification" or defense of Zeus' accession to cosmic rule, relates most readily to Milton's specifically divine argument. The *Theogony*'s great concerns, cosmogony and the revolt in heaven, are paralleled and reinterpreted in the central books of *Paradise Lost.* (I shall turn to consider the latter in detail in a moment.)

Milton saw in Hesiod, then, not only a classical prototype of the divinely inspired poet, but simultaneously a poet who had dealt with the very matters to which Moses had addressed himself and which Milton aimed to treat again. By alluding to both these aspects of Hesiod's significance in *Paradise Lost*'s proem, Milton urges the inseparability of inspiration and content. An almost incidental passage in *Il Penseroso* adumbrates Hesiod's meaning for Milton later in the great epic; he is addressing Melancholy:

> And join with thee calm Peace, and Quiet,
> Spare Fast, that oft with gods doth diet,
> And hears the Muses in a ring
> Ay round about Jove's altar sing.
>
> (45–48)

The young Milton, still in his poetic apprenticeship, is recalling a striking image from the first lines of the *Theogony:*

> Μουσάων Ἑλικωνιάδων ἀρχώμεθ᾽ ἀείδειν,
> αἵθ᾽ Ἑλικῶνος ἔχουσιν ὄρος μέγα τε ζάθεόν τε
> καί τε περὶ κρήνην ἰοειδέα πόσσ᾽ ἁπαλοῖσιν
> ὀρχεῦνται καὶ βωμὸν ἐρισθενέος Κρονίωνος.
>
> (1–4)

> (Let us begin our song with the Heliconian Muses, who
> hold the great and sacred mountain of Helicon, and
> who with soft feet dance about the violet spring and the
> altar of the mighty son of Kronos.)

For Milton, these lines appear to have emblematized poetic inspiration in service to God. Hesiod would not have caviled at this interpretation.

Herodotus commented (2.53) that Homer and Hesiod had given the Greeks their gods. The contrast between the elaborate catalogues of deities in the *Theogony* and the fundamentally human narratives of the *Iliad* and *Odyssey* suggests, at least to the modern reader, that Hesiod was a more single-minded theologian than Homer. Nevertheless, we are surely safe in assuming that Milton would not have scrupled to damn them in tandem. In his comments upon Hesiod in the *De poetarum historia* (Basel, 1580), often reprinted with the prefatory matter to late sixteenth-century and early seventeenth-century editions of Hesiod, such as those of Schrevelius (London, 1601), Lilio Giraldi reports out of Lucian that Hesiod and Homer both fried in hell for having spoken falsely about the gods. It would appear that if he could undermine Homeric heroic ideals in his epic narrative and Hesiodic theology in his invocatory prologues, Milton would clear Christian poetry root and branch of the falsehoods that had persisted from the classical tradition. Conventional interpretations of Milton's classicism incline us to presume that he has daringly compared Hesiod to both Moses and himself in order to render all the more pointed the differences between the true paradigm of inspiration and the false. But it is not so simple.

We shall leave Homer to fend for himself. Hesiod, for his part, strenuously resists being drafted as a champion of the untruths of pagan religion. He reports the Muses' startling disclosure that they can both disguise the false to seem real and also speak the truth when they desire:

> ποιμένες ἄγραυλοι, κάκ' ἐλέγχεα, γαστέρες οἶον,
> ἴδμεν ψεύδεα πολλὰ λέγειν ἐτύμοισιν ὁμοῖα,
> ἴδμεν δ', εὖτ' ἐθέλωμεν, ἀληθέα γηρύσασθαι.
>
> (*Theogony* 26–28)

> (Shepherds whose home is in the wilds, you miserable disgraces to your trade, all bellies, we know how to tell many falsehoods that seem real: but we also know how to speak truth when we wish to.)

Classicists are far from unanimous in their understanding
of these lines. The self-recommending antagonism to other
possible traditions that seems apparent in these lines is hard
to reconcile with the dominant modern notion that Hesiod's
poetry, like Homer's, arises out of a quasi-tribal tradition that
does not—indeed, cannot—stand in opposition to its own cultural context and, further, is not likely to recognize a plurality
of traditions among which one can choose. But Pietro Pucci
has affirmed that the apparent meaning is at least partly correct:

> Although the concept of the Muses' inspiration may hint
> at the existence of a poetic tradition, Hesiod belittles his
> debt to it by describing his own uniquely privileged inti-
> macy with the Muses. They often lie to their devotees, but
> not, presumably, to Hesiod. The awareness of this exclusive-
> ness dictates the pungent insults that Hesiod, through the
> Muses, addresses to his fellow poets, both his predecessors
> and contemporary singers.[10]

Robert Herrick quotes the Muses' distinction between merely
apparent and genuine truth as the epigraph to his *Noble Numbers*.[11] The clear implication is that the secular trivia of *Hesperi-
des*—published a year later but mostly written much earlier—
had been of the first type of inspiration, while the divine
poems of *Noble Numbers* presented truth itself. Such a Christian reading of these lines would have been obvious to Milton,
too. St. Peter's abusive address in *Lycidas* echoes *Theogony* 26,
and although Milton does not allude to the next two lines as
well (those quoted by Herrick), the contexts are apposite:

> How well could I have spared for thee, young swain,
> Enow of such as for their bellies' sake,
> Creep and intrude, and climb into the fold?

. . . .
Blind mouths! that scarce themselves know how to hold
A sheep-hook, or have learned aught else the least
That to the faithful herdman's art belongs!

(*Lycidas* 113–15, 119–21)

Hesiod was, moreover, distinguished specifically from Homer by a late classical work, *The Contest of Homer and Hesiod,* which Milton may have known from Daniel Heinsius's elaborate edition of Hesiod (1603). In this narrative, after much improvisational sparring during which the audience's applause favors Homer, Hesiod is awarded the prize, because, as the judge explains, it was right that the man who celebrated the arts of agriculture and peace should be preferred to the man who celebrated war.[12] Milton probably would not have regarded it as credible history, but the legend's lesson could hardly have failed to strike in him a responsive chord.

The antitraditionalism of Hesiod's proem calls to mind the same quality in Milton's prologues, and ironically what began here as an attempt to authenticate Milton's inspiration by contrast to the false or inadequate inspiration of Hesiod brings us to confess only that the evidence provided by the poems is inadequate to such a distinction. The purpose of the conventional invocation, exemplified by the brief appeals of Homer and Vergil, is to ally the poet with the tradition from which what he is about to say derives its authority, that is, its prestige, its persuasiveness, or, most basically, its claim to the reader's or auditor's attention.[13] But Hesiod and Milton alike flout convention. Rather than take the initiative themselves by calling upon the Muses, they affirm that the Muses have elected to call upon them. In other words, they derive their vatic authority from *vocation* rather than *invocation.* To be sure, invocation is not absent from their poetry, but it is curiously undermined. The

Theogony's invocation (104–15) occurs only after an extended hymn to the Muses, in which is narrated first their nocturnal epiphany to Hesiod and election of him as their hierophant, and second, their birth, demonstrating thus before the invocation that the poet already knows them intimately and that, in short, they have answered his prayer before he has framed it. Milton, as is his wont, inverts his classical model. Rather than a lengthy account of his vocation followed by a brief prayer, he presents first, as the prologues to books 1, 3, and 7 of *Paradise Lost*, three lengthy but increasingly diffident prayers, the last of which closes plaintively, "So fail not thou, who thee implores" (7.38); but these are undercut finally by the prologue to book 9, which is not an invocation at all and in which he tells how his Celestial Patroness "deigns / Her nightly visitation unimplored" (9.21–22).[14] This does not exactly mean, of course, that the invocations that preceded were supererogatory. The grand ambition revealed there testifies to the poet's desire to make himself deserving of the Muse's revelation. And so she finds him: "She *deigns.* . . ."[15]

So Hesiod turns *Paradise Lost*'s critique back upon itself: Milton would reject the ancient poet that he most resembles. There are perhaps some for whom the authentication of Milton's inspiration requires only weighing the Christianity of *Paradise Lost* against the paganism of the *Theogony*. But this drives the reader to a kind of literalism that I suspect many of us would not find congenial; piety here is hard to distinguish from chauvinism. One critic, William Kerrigan, concludes that the reader must simply take a stand on Milton's inspiration. At the beginning of *The Prophetic Milton*, Kerrigan says bafflingly, "I assume throughout this study that I do in fact believe in prophetic inspiration."[16] I think Kerrigan is quite right to eschew the historically sophisticated pretense of much criticism, but he himself simply defers our examination of what we had thought was the problem, namely, how seriously to take the poet's pretense to inspiration, and forces us to wonder instead how seriously to take the critic's pretense to belief. He never explains what this "inspiration" is or what his belief in it means; nor does he provide a criterion by which we can discriminate true from false inspiration. We are asked then to take a stand on a mystery, and the correct understanding of *Paradise Lost* becomes a *res fidei*. Perhaps this is simply in the nature of poetry. Pucci discovers in *Theogony* 26–28 a dilemma for both reader and poet: the lines seem to promise truth, but the Muses do not disclose to Hesiod the criterion by which he could distinguish genuine and merely apparent truth.[17] And yet, because these poems deal with matters of utmost consequence, we cannot afford to disregard the issue that they make of their own truthfulness. It is what is at stake that distinguishes the heroic irony of Milton and Hesiod from the comic irony of Chaucer or the epistemological teasing of the fictions of Apuleius and Borges and Nabokov. If we cannot confidently authenticate Milton's claims (or Hesiod's), neither can we afford to take them lightly.

Hesiod's Titanomachy

The *Works and Days* appears to have been more popular in the Renaissance than the *Theogony,* and Milton's own recommendation of Hesiod as a school text in the essay "Of Education" appears to have been directed at the *Works and Days* specifically.[18] Milton's poetic references to the *Works and Days* demonstrate a close acquaintance with the text. For example, with *Paradise Lost* 2.841–42 (the peregrinations of Sin and Death), compare *Works and Days* 102–4 (the comings and goings of the Diseases); and, perhaps as a complement to the preceding allusion, with *Paradise Lost* 4.677–78 ("spiritual creatures" walking the Earth), compare *Works and Days* 124–25 (spirit guardians). One of Todd's authorities refers *Paradise Lost* 10.304–5, a "passage broad, / Smooth, easy, inoffensive down to Hell," to *Works and Days* 287–88, "Badness can be had abundantly and with ease; the path to her is smooth [λείη]." If this is a genuine borrowing—and it is as plausible verbally and contextually as many another—it is evidence of the meticulous attention Milton had granted the text of Hesiod. I have found no edition that recognizes the variant λείη, "smooth," on which the association of these two passages heavily depends, before that of Graevius (Amsterdam, 1667), whose text indeed retains ὀλίγη, "short," the unanimous reading of the manuscripts, but who cites Plato's reading λείη (*Republic* 364c, and again *Laws* 718e) as preferable in the accompanying commentary on the text.

The overwhelming preponderance of Milton's allusions to the *Theogony*, then, is striking. When we consider further that (apart from these prologues) these allusions are aimed almost exclusively at the titanomachy and its immediate aftermath, we may begin to recognize how calculatedly Milton has engaged Hesiod here. Milton's war in heaven, of course, had numerous specific precedents besides Hesiod's titanomachy.[19] More generally, the martial dimension of the entire epic tradition is called to account in *Paradise Lost* 6, perhaps especially Homer's theomachy in *Iliad* 21 and 22.[20] But no other single work is alluded to in *Paradise Lost* 6 so extensively or to such purpose as the *Theogony*. The rejection of the Hesiodic paradigm of inspiration elaborated in *Paradise Lost*'s prologues is complemented by a critique of pagan theology implied by means of a careful reworking of the *Theogony*'s climactic episode—what Wilamowitz called the "showpiece" of the poem. It was this battle that brought Zeus to rule.

It is important to notice how carefully Milton in his earlier

books sets up the ambush he makes on Hesiod in book 6.
There are three allusions to the *Theogony* in books 1 and 2.
They are notable enough in themselves, but what is striking
about them in ensemble is the way they work sequentially
through a single passage, *Theogony* 720–743, a description of
Tartarus accompanying the narrative of the titans' imprison-
ment. The first of these allusions is pointed out by most of
Milton's recent annotators, but it is often misunderstood:

> Him the almighty power
> Hurled headlong flaming from the ethereal sky
> With hideous ruin and combustion down
> To bottomless perdition, there to dwell
> In adamantine chains and penal fire,
> Who durst defy the omnipotent to arms.
> Nine times the space that measures day and night
> To mortal men, he with his horrid crew
> Lay vanquished, rolling in the fiery gulf
> Confounded though immortal.
>
> (1.44–53)

These lines in themselves do not constitute an allusion to
Hesiod, as is sometimes claimed.[21] Their significance is not
complete until one associates them with line 871 of book 6,
which states specifically *how long* it took for the rebel angels to
fall from heaven: nine days. After their defeat, Hesiod's titans
were confined to Tartarus, which he says is as far beneath the
Earth as heaven is above, and he specifies this distance:

> ἐννέα γὰρ νύκτας τε καὶ ἤματα χάλκεος ἄκμων,
> οὐρανόθεν κατιὼν δεκάτῃ κ᾽ ἐς γαῖαν ἵκοιτο·
> ἐννέα δ᾽ αὖ νύκτας τε καὶ ἤματα χάλκεος ἄκμων
> ἐκ γαίης κατιὼν δεκάτῃ κ᾽ ἐς Τάρταρον ἵκοι.
>
> (722–25)[22]

(a bronze anvil dropping from heaven for nine nights
and days would come to the earth on the tenth; likewise, a bronze anvil dropping from the earth for nine
nights and days would come to Tartarus on the tenth.)

The twice nine days for which Hesiod's anvil plummets are
broken up by Milton before being applied to his rebel angels
(nine days falling and nine more "rolling in the fiery gulf").
The division was forced upon him by his cosmology: in the
universe of *Paradise Lost* the path from heaven to hell does
not go by Earth. These are respectively Milton's first and final
allusions to the text of the *Theogony* and serve to enclose his
reworking of the titanomachy. This sort of double allusion is a
technique of special emphasis used sparingly by Milton. The
other major one—to *Aeneid* 1.11, "tantaene animis caelestibus
irae?"–will be considered in the next chapter.

In book 2, Milton continues his reworking of *Theogony* 720–
43 with two allusions.

> at last appear
> Hell bounds high reaching to the horrid roof,
> And thrice threefold the gates; three folds were brass,
> Three iron, three of adamantine rock,
> Impenetrable, impaled with circling fire,
> Yet unconsumed.
>
> (2.643–48)

In reference to this, the first of the pair, Bishop Stillingfleet
(in Newton) adduces *Theogony* 726–33:

> Τὸν πέρι χάλκεον ἕρκος ἐλήλαται· ἀμφὶ δέ μιν νὺξ
> τριστοιχὶ κέχυται περὶ δειρήν· αὐτὰρ ὕπερθεν
> γῆς ῥίζαι πεφύασι καὶ ἀτρυγέτοιο θαλάσσης.
> ἔνθα θεοὶ Τιτῆνες ὑπὸ ζόφῳ ἠερόεντι
> κεκρύφαται βουλῇσι Διὸς νεφεληγερέταο   730

χώρῳ ἐν εὐρώεντι, πελώρης ἔσχατα γαίης.
τοῖς οὐκ ἐξιτόν ἐστι. θύρας δ' ἐπέθηκε Ποσειδέων
χαλκείας, τεῖχος δὲ περοίχεται ἀμφοτέρωθεν.

(726–33)

(A bronze fence stretches around Tartarus, and about its
throat spills threefold night; but above grow the roots
of earth and of the barren sea. There beneath the misty
gloom the titan gods are hidden according to the plan
of cloud-gathering Zeus, in a dank place, at the end of
the huge earth. They cannot go out. Poseidon has set up
bronze gates and a wall runs about it on both sides.)

Note that these lines follow immediately upon those targeted
in the previous allusion (*Paradise Lost* 1.50 to *Theogony* 722–
25). Here Milton has outdone Hesiod's "threefold" (τριστοιχὶ,
727) with his "thrice threefold,"[23] although, if I may be permitted to speak in the manner of the eighteenth-century scholars, I will say that his arithmetical superiority here has not
bought him an improvement on Hesiod's fine passage. (The
ambiguity of περὶ δειρήν 727, "about its throat," is especially
beautiful.) The other allusion in book 2 likewise continues to
follow Hesiod's description of Tartarus.[24] It is, says Hesiod,

χάσμα μέγ', οὐδέ κε πάντα τελεσφόρον εἰς ἐνιαυτὸν
οὖδας ἵκοιτ', εἰ πρῶτα πυλέων ἔντοσθε γένοιτο,
ἀλλά κεν ἔνθα καὶ ἔνθα φέροι πρὸ θύελλα θυέλλης
ἀργαλέη.

(740–43)

(a great chasm: a man wouldn't reach the bottom for an
entire year if he came to be within its gates, but would
be borne here and there by whirlwind upon harsh
whirlwind.)

Todd notes the allusion at *Paradise Lost* 2.931–38, where Satan, exiting from Hell,

> meets
> A vast vacuity: all unawares
> Fluttering his pennons vain plumb down he drops
> Ten thousand fathom deep, and to this hour
> Down had been falling, had not by ill chance
> The strong rebuff of some tumultuous cloud
> Instinct with fire and nitre hurried him
> As many miles aloft.
>
> (2.931–38)

The gusts are significantly Hesiodic: M. L. West, Hesiod's great modern commentator, notes at 742 that in Homer, Tartarus is windless (*Iliad* 8.481). Here, too, Milton amplifies and embellishes his model, this time to his credit. His "vast vacuity" exactly translates Hesiod's χάσμα μέγ' (740). Note also that while Hesiod's unfortunate man is just *within* the gates of Tartarus, Satan is just *outside* the gates of Hell (see 884, and compare with 918). It is characteristic of Milton's genuine allusions that some detail in the target passage be inverted or undercut. Although neither of the allusions in book 2 is of crucial significance in itself, their orderliness is indicative of the care with which Milton is attending to Hesiod's poem and prepares one for the critical maneuvers of book 6.

As we saw, one does not have to read far into the first book of *Paradise Lost*—only fifty lines—for Milton's first allusion to the text of the *Theogony*. Book 6, where Hesiod is most important, heralds its concern with that poem even more promptly:

> There is a cave
> Within the mount of God, fast by his throne,
> Where light and darkness in perpetual round

Lodge and dislodge by turns, which makes through
    heaven
Grateful vicissitude, like day and night;
Light issues forth, and at the other door
Obsequious darkness enters, till her hour
To veil the heaven, though darkness there might
    well
Seem twilight here.

(6.4–12)

Newton, Milton's greatest eighteenth-century commentator, observes that this is "plainly borrowed from a fine passage in Hesiod," and quotes *Theogony* 748–51. Let me quote a slightly larger passage, to make the correspondence to Milton's passage clearer:

Νυκτὸς δ᾽ ἐρεβεννῆς οἰκία δεινὰ
ἕστηκεν νεφέλης κεκαλυμμένα κυανέῃσιν.
τῶν πρόσθ᾽ Ἰαπετοῖο πάις ἔχει οὐρανὸν εὐρὺν
ἑστηὼς κεφαλῇ τε καὶ ἀκαμάτῃσι χέρεσσιν
ἀστεμφέως, ὅθι Νύξ τε καὶ Ἡμέρη ἆσσον ἰοῦσαι
ἀλλήλας προσέειπον, ἀμειβόμεναι μέγαν οὐδὸν
χάλκεον· ἣ μὲν ἔσω καταβήσεται, ἣ δὲ θύραζε
ἔρχεται, οὐδέ ποτ᾽ ἀμφοτέρας δόμος ἐντὸς ἐέργει,
ἀλλ᾽ αἰεὶ ἑτέρη γε δόμων ἔκτοσθεν ἐοῦσα
γαῖαν ἐπιστρέφεται, ἣ δ᾽ αὖ δόμου ἐντὸς ἐοῦσα
μίμνει τὴν αὐτῆς ὥρην ὁδοῦ, ἔστ᾽ ἂν ἵκηται.

(744–754)

(The awesome home of murky Night stands hidden in deep blue clouds. In front of them Iapetus' son stands motionless, supporting wide heaven on his head and tireless hands; there Night and Day come close and greet one another as they pass in and out over the great

> bronze threshold. One goes down into the house, as
> the other comes out the door; never are both within
> the house at once, but one always stays outside, ranging
> over the earth, and the other stays ever inside, waiting
> until the time for her journey arrive.)

This passage follows directly upon the description of Tartarus where Milton left it at his last allusion in book 2—but one thing is crucially different. As long as his scene was set at the lower frontier of the universe (Hell and Chaos), the context of Milton's lines was directly analogous to the context of the lines alluded to in the *Theogony*. But here at the beginning of book 6, the analogy between the contexts is inverted: Milton's cave of light and darkness is placed in heaven, while Hesiod's is located indefinitely in the nether world; and while Hesiod brings his reader to the home of Night in the aftermath of the celestial battle, Milton's description of the cave *precedes* it. It is a pivotal allusion. Milton has reached this point by following the text of the *Theogony* closely, from 720–21, to 726–27, to 740–41, to the home of Night at 744–45. But now he will turn back in his text—or his memory—to the beginning of the titanomachy. Henceforth he will abandon his attention to sequence. Another principle of order is now at work.

Throughout the first two days of the battle, Milton alludes repeatedly to the titanomachy. Most of these allusions, like most of his Biblical references, are borrowings, not strong allusions. None is crucial in itself, but in accumulation they give necessary support to the handful of strong allusions by which he strikes to the heart of Hesiod's text. Milton is generally more interested in *what* Hesiod says than in *how* he says it, and on the whole the technique of his martial narrative is roughly Homeric or Vergilian. But this passage, with its flurry of weak allusions, is unmistakably Hesiodic even where it does not specifically correspond to anything in the titanomachy. Milton is describing the beginning of the melée after Abdiel's bout with Satan:

> nor stood at gaze
> The adverse legions, nor less hideous joined
> The horrid shock: now storming fury rose,
> And clamour such as heard in heaven till now
> Was never, arms on armour clashing brayed
> Horrible discord, and the madding wheels   210
> Of brazen chariots raged; dire was the noise
> Of conflict; over head the dismal hiss
> Of fiery darts in flaming volleys flew,
> And flying vaulted either host with fire.
> So under fiery cope together rushed   215
> Both battles main, with ruinous assault
> And inextinguishable rage; all heaven
> Resounded, and had earth been then, all earth
> Had to her centre shook.

(6.205–19)

This is how Hesiod's theogonic broil commences:

> Τιτῆνες δ᾽ ἑτέρωθεν ἐκαρτύναντο φάλαγγας
> προφρονέως· χειρῶν τε βίης θ᾽ ἅμα ἔργον ἔφαινον
> ἀμφότεροι. δεινὸν δὲ περίαχε πόντος ἀπείρων,
> γῆ δὲ μέγ᾽ ἐσμαράγησεν, ἐπέστενε δ᾽ οὐρανὸς εὐρὺς
> σειόμενος, πεδόθεν δὲ τινάσσετο μακρὸς Ὄλυμπος 680
> ῥιπῇ ὕπ᾽ ἀθανάτων, ἔνοσις δ᾽ ἵκανε βαρεῖα
> Τάρταρον ἠερόεντα ποδῶν, αἰπεῖά τ᾽ ἰωὴ
> ἀσπέτου ἰωχμοῖο βολάων τε κρατεράων.
> ὣς ἄρ᾽ ἐπ᾽ ἀλλήλοις ἵεσαν βέλεα στονόεντα·

φωνὴ δ᾽ ἀμφοτέρων ἵκετ᾽ οὐρανὸν ἀστερόεντα
κεκλομένων· οἳ δὲ ξύνισαν μεγάλῳ ἀλαλητῷ.

(676–86)

(The titans on the other side strengthened their ranks
with a will, and both sides displayed at one time the
work of their mighty hands. The boundless sea clam-
ored terribly about and the earth crashed grandly; the
broad heaven moaned as it shook, and great Olympus
quaked from beneath because of the immortals' charge.
The deep shaking caused by their footsteps reached
gloomy Tartarus, as did the shrill noise of the inexpres-
sible battle din and of mighty spears. This is how it was
when they threw their cruel shafts at one another. The
sound of both sides' outcry reached the starry heaven;
they came together with a great war whoop.)

Both poets emphasize the din of celestial conflict. In each case
the scene is, without hyperbole, one of cosmic cataclysm. The
individual combatants are rarified out of existence; nothing
remains but the visceral sensations of noise and quaking.
Milton's panorama admits a degree of visual perspective
("wheels of brazen chariots," "fiery darts") unavailable to
Hesiod, for Raphael was an eyewitness to the events he narrates. But this is a slight difference. Both scenes are more
symphonic here than cinematic.

Milton anticipates himself here in one or two particulars.
The shaking at lines 218–19 looks forward to lines 832–34,
where Messiah rides forth in his chariot:

> under his burning wheels
> The steadfast empyrean shook throughout,
> All but the throne it self of God.

(832–34)

Here Milton is recalling the shaking of heaven and Tartarus at the beginning of the titanomachy, as well as, perhaps, the shaking of Olympus as Zeus rises against Typhoeus (*Theogony* 842–43, outside the titanomachy, but a kind of double of it). And the fighting beneath the "fiery cope" (215) looks forward to the end of the angelic battle on the second day, when the angels pluck up hills (644–45; compare with *Theogony* 675) and throw them through the air at the dumbfounded rebels so that "under ground they fought in dismal shade" (666). With this compare the conclusion of Hesiod's battle, when the hundred-handers launched their huge rocks and "overshadowed the titans with their missiles" (κατὰ δ᾽ ἐσκίασαν βελέεσσι / Τιτῆνας, 716–17).[25]

These borrowings or weak allusions set up the broad analogy between Hesiod's war in heaven and Milton's war. The few strong allusions, however, the striking points of Milton's poetic revision of Hesiod, are aimed to explode the analogy by controverting the reader's facile inference that, just because the rebel angels resemble the titans (as the defeated and fallen), Messiah must resemble Zeus. But Milton's stratagem, I shall argue, is equally facile. He pulls the reader up short simply by attributing to *Satan* rather than to Messiah the proper virtue of Zeus, which may be regarded as the combination of knowledge with power.

In the *Theogony*, Zeus' surpassing excellence, his ἀρετή, consists in his wisdom or intelligence rather than his strength, as Kottos, being appealed to for help, admits: "We know that you excel in understanding and thought" (656). What really makes Zeus "best of gods and greatest in might" (49) is that he prudently makes as many and as powerful alliances as he can. Hesiod refers prominently to these at the beginning of the poem (73–74, and again at 112), and their importance is the lesson of the episode concerning Styx (389–403).

Zeus owes his weapons, the lightning and thunderbolts, to the Cyclopes. The weapons with which he crushes Typhoeus (854)—although here at least he appears to be on his own—bear the very names of the Cyclopes (compare with 140). And he overcomes the titans only after having gained the assistance of the hundred-handers, whose physiques clearly symbolize unrestrainable force. Zeus is more of a general than a champion combatant, that is, more Agamemnon than Achilles, and more of a politician than either. "But he himself wields power and greatly rules" (403) is a compliment that does not pierce the surface of Zeus' "public image."

In book 6 Milton permits Satan and Messiah to characterize their own actions in terms that are quite contrary to those we know to be appropriate. This ironic role-swapping is designed to suggest—contrary to the reader's expectations—an analogy between Zeus and Satan. Satan, for his part, boasts of invincibility through "strength and counsel joined" (6.494). Messiah, on the other hand, routs his adversaries single-handedly, and ironically he chooses to do so not by means of his superior virtue or intelligence, but by force alone:

> That they may have their wish, to try with me
> In battle which the stronger proves, they all,
> Or I alone against them, since by strength
> They measure all, of other excellence
> Not emulous, nor care who them excels.
>
> (6.818–22)

Here Milton is not even being fair to his own characters. Satan *claims* at least to be "emulous of other excellence." He is proud of his intelligence, which even in book 1 (after the battle) he deems equal to the Son's:

> furthest from him is best
> Whom reason hath equalled, force hath made supreme
> Above his equals.
>
> (1.247–49; compare with 1.256–58)

And later in the same book, Satan's lines are compelling indeed, taken in themselves:

> our better part remains
> To work in close design, by fraud or guile
> What force effected not: that he no less
> At length from us may find, who overcomes
> By force, hath overcome but half his foe.
>
> (1.645–49)

Of course, he is tragically deluded. Milton's oblique analogy with Hesiod indicates that he could see perfectly well what the Greek poet was trying to do. He simply contradicts the *Theogony* by implying that Zeus' knowledge is as fraudulent as Satan's and his regime a tyranny based solely on force.

Actually, Hesiod takes pains to express Zeus' grandeur and power while at the same time insulating him from the exercise of brute force that finally overcomes the titans. Zeus is not given a specific opponent in the battle: his *aristeia* (687–710) is not so much a combat as a spectacular fireworks display. The dirty work, meanwhile, is taken care of by his henchmen (713–19). Hesiod was eager to believe, we may be sure, that Zeus ruled the universe not simply because he was mightier than anyone else, but because he was an intrinsically superior kind of being. One finds in Hesiod no trace of the myth that Zeus won Olympus from his brothers by lot. Homer's portrayal of Zeus in this way (see *Iliad* 15.189–93) should have scandalized Hesiod.

Now Milton would have us think that *he* is scandalized by *Hesiod*. But his concern is Hesiod's own, precisely: to allay the suspicion that only superior force keeps God on his throne. And yet he manages to turn the tables on Hesiod here. He has prompted his "fit reader" to link Satan with Zeus; but he also anticipates and provides for the general reader's natural temptation to compare the Greek god to the Christian.[26] Thyer (one of Newton's auxiliaries) could not resist:

> The description of the Messiah's going out against the rebel Angels is a scene of the same sort with Hesiod's Jupiter against the Titans. They are both of them the most undoubted instances of the true sublime; but which has exceeded it is very difficult to determine. There is, I think, a greater profusion of poetical images in that of the latter; but then the superiour character of a Christian Messiah, which Milton has, with great judgment and majesty, supported in this part of his work, gives a certain air of religious grandeur, which throws the advantage on the side of the English poet.   (*Poetical Works of John Milton*, ed. Todd, at 6.746)

In other words, Hesiod would have won on points, but Milton knocked him out. The real trick is that he does it by pulling his punch. Messiah claims that he will meet force with force, but he does not really do so. His intrinsic virtue is infinitely superior to that of any of the angels, and when he shows himself to the rebels, they are awe-struck and routed at once. His terrible and mysterious majesty

> withered all their strength,
> And of their wonted vigor left them drained,
> Exhausted, spiritless, afflicted, fallen.
> Yet *half his strength he put not forth.*
>   (6.850–53, emphasis added)

He scarcely soils his hands. Milton's use of "half his strength" is precisely calculated. Zeus' *aristeia*, the climax of the entire *Theogony*, begins:

Οὐδ᾽ ἄρ᾽ ἔτι Ζεὺς ἴσχεν ἑὸν μένος, ἀλλά νυ τοῦ γε
εἶθαρ μὲν μένεος πλῆντο φρένες, ἐκ δέ τε πᾶσαν
φαῖνε βίην.

(687–89)

(Then Zeus no longer checked his might, but might at once filled his heart and *he showed forth all his strength.*)
[emphasis added]

It is worth noting that Milton's iteration of key words ("strength . . . vigor . . . strength") imitates Hesiod's ("might . . . might . . . strength"). But the main spark of the allusion, of course, leaps between the lines that I have emphasized. Milton invites one to meditate on the contrast between the Greek god, exerting himself to the limit against no one in particular and succeeding in the end only with the aid of the monstrous hundred-handers, and the Christian Messiah, who faces the entire rebel army and defeats them almost without trying. In this simple, but strong, allusion is to be found the denouement of Milton's putative critique of Hesiod and thus of Greek myth generally, the culmination of the subtle inversion signalled by the first allusion in book 6.

Horace's "Descende caelo"

Bishop Newton was the first to note that the opening words of *Paradise Lost* 7, "Descend from heaven," translate the opening words of one of Horace's great odes (3.4), "Descende caelo." It is, as I shall argue, a crucial allusion, yet to my knowledge no one has ever seen more than a cursory borrowing here.

Beyond the opening words, the precise verbal similarities of the two passages are admittedly slight, and I imagine the fact that the original here is a lyric poem rather than an epic has had something to do with the allusion's having been largely overlooked. On the other hand, although not much attention has ever been given to lyrical influences on *Paradise Lost,* the poem's debts to the dramatic tradition, to give only one example, have been acknowledged (and then some), and the persistent prejudice against generic impurity exhibited by most modern studies of Milton's classicism owes more to Renaissance critical theory than to actual poetic practice.[27] I suspect a deeper reason that Horace's importance has been missed is that Milton's tag, "Descend from heaven," and the rest of the prologue to book 7 have been mistaken to connote simply a religious concern that is in no way paralleled in Horace's ode. But Milton's allusion to Horace is complementary to his earlier allusions to Hesiod, to whom Horace himself alludes in this poem. Hesiod provides the theological burden and Horace the political counterpoint.

"Descende caelo" was written around 28 B.C., soon after Octavian's retirement from the civil war's second phase, the power struggle with Antony. At eighty lines, it is the longest of Horace's odes; he himself calls it a "longum . . . melos" (2). It is fourth in the sequence of six so-called Roman Odes that opens book 3. These are strongly bound together (as well as set off from the odes immediately following in that book) by their common Alcaic meter, inordinate length, serious social and political themes, and subtle cross-references. The sequence is as close to epic as Horace ever got or (I am sure) wanted to get—close enough to mitigate the generic impurity of Milton's allusion. There are, in fact, various thematic affinities between the Roman Odes and *Paradise Lost* apart from those implied in the allusion to *Descende caelo*. For example, Horace's claim in the first ode to sing "songs never heard before" (2–3) is one of several classical instances of the originality *topos* that echo in Milton's "Things unattempted yet in prose or rhyme" (1.16). Abdiel, the lone dissenter among Satan's squadrons in book 5, comes readily to mind when one reads Horace's portrait, at the beginning of the third ode, of the solitary man of justice who is not shaken from what he knows is right by the mob of his misled fellow citizens or the threatening scowl of the tyrant. The curious may discover for themselves more parallels of this sort.

The fourth ode's eighty lines break neatly into two parts, whose juncture is a matter of some subtlety, if not sleight of hand. In the first half of the poem, Horace invokes the muse Calliope (1–8) and then relates at length the special care with which she and her sisters have watched over him throughout his life. People marveled, he says, at how as a boy he slept in the woods safe from snakes and bears: "Non sine dis animosus infans" (20: "with divine assistance, a fearless, inspired child").[28] As an adult, too, the friendship of the Muses has made him inviolable, proof against reverses in battle, falling trees, and shipwreck (25–28). If the Muses are with him, there is no place he would not dare to go. Why, he would even visit the inhospitable English (29–36)! At the crux of the poem, the point of transition from the invocatory first half to what we shall see is a catastrophic second half, the poet leaves himself behind, and the Muses are linked instead with Caesar:

> uos Caesarem altum, militia simul
> fessas cohortis abdidit oppidis,
>   finire quaerentem labores
>   Pierio recreatis antro.

uos lene consilium et datis et dato
gaudetis almae.

(37–4?)

(In a Pierian grotto you refresh the exalted Caesar, who,
eager to put an end to his labors, has just tucked away
in the towns his battle-weary regiments. You give gentle
counsel and rejoice in having given it.)

Horace goes on, looking back in time, to characterize the
wickedness of the Antonians by alluding to the mythical titans
and giants who assailed heaven (42–64) and moralizing: "uis
consili expers mole ruit sua" (65: "force without counsel is its
own undoing"). The final three stanzas (69–80) recall the terrible punishments meted out to several mythic exemplars of
incontinence. The tone of these final lines is elegiac, not cen-
sorious. Earth grieves, he says, for her offspring whom she
herself imprisons; three hundred chains bind the wretched
lover Pirithous. The images connote with the utmost delicacy
the tragedy of civil war. Pirithous, once companion of the hero
Theseus, is an allegory for Antony, at one time Octavian's ally;
and Earth, mother of giants, is no less mother of us all. The
sympathy elicited here for the poet's and reader's defeated
fellow citizens works back upon earlier stanzas. The "lene consilium" now is seen to be clemency; on the other hand, "uis
consili expers mole ruit sua," which one takes at first as an
almanac proverb, seems on reflection more meaningful for
Augustus than for the titans. At the end of the ode, we feel
that we have come a long way from the beginning and we are
not even quite sure how. But the first half's autobiographical
romance serves rhetorically to enhance the poet's *auctoritas* in
preparation for his political rumination.[29]

Milton's allusion is homologous to *Descende caelo* with respect both to book and line. The ode, which comes fourth in book 3, occupies the same position relative to the six-ode sequence of Roman odes as does Milton's book 7 relative to *Paradise Lost*'s twelve books: each comes first in the second half.[30] And the correspondence of first line to first line is especially conspicuous. Classically oriented poets as diverse as Ariosto, Spenser, Milton, and Pope exhibit a fondness for such analogously placed allusions at the beginnings or, less often, the ends of books.[31] The technique had the sanction of Vergil, who in the *Aeneid*'s first line alludes to the first lines of both the *Iliad* and the *Odyssey*.[32] More relevant to my present concern is the fact that Horace, too, uses the technique in several of his reworkings of Greek lyrics.[33] Milton follows his example in the very Horatian Sonnet 20, whose first line, "Lawrence of virtuous father virtuous son," alludes to the first line of *Odes* 1.16, "O matre pulchra filia pulchrior." Typically the precise verbal similarity between Horace's ode and its model dissolves after the first line or two, however extensive the two poems' thematic affinities. It is not impossible that the brevity of Milton's verbal allusion at *Paradise Lost* 7.1 is precisely a Horatian *jeu d'esprit*. I suppose this is a kind of intertextual litotes: the effect intended was emphasis by understatement.

Milton reworks both of the ode's themes, but (in typical epic fashion) in reverse order. In the prologue to *Paradise Lost* 7 (thirty-nine lines) he reworks the theme of the ode's first half (forty lines): the Muse's protection of the poet. To be sure, his treatment of the theme is more complex than Horace's; it has a negative as well as a positive aspect. Milton, like Horace, is concerned with dramatizing the perils he himself has faced and continues to face. He affirms that the Muse has kept him "safe" (15, 24) despite the extraordinary difficulties and even dangers of his poetic undertaking. But at the end of the prologue he turns to lament Calliope's failure to save her poet-son Orpheus, as he had done decades earlier in *Lycidas*. This negative exemplum would seem to put the lie to Horace's confident claim to the Muse's patronage, for the rejected, impotent Muse here is Horace's "regina . . . Calliope" (3.4.2), displaced from the beginning of the prologue to make room for Urania. The final line of the prologue, "For thou art heavenly, she an empty dream" (39), looks back to line 1 to undercut Horace's prayer, "descende caelo," by exposing Horace's "heaven" as nothing more than the "Olympian hill" above which Milton soars.

His reworking of the ode's other main theme occurs immediately prior to the overt allusion at 7.1, in *Paradise Lost* 6, where he narrates the war in heaven. The primary classical authority here for his narrative considered *in extenso* is Hesiod's account of the titanomachy in the *Theogony*, which was considered earlier. But for Milton's purposes, Horace's brief scenes of celestial revolt provide a crucial thematic complement to Hesiod's narrative. Horace's striking contribution here is the interpretation of the revolt in heaven in current political terms. Like Milton, Horace was writing his poem soon after the collapse of republican government and the "restoration" of monarchy.[34] His picture of the titan and giant rebellions, like Milton's representation of the angelic revolt, calls to mind the civil war just concluded in his country.

In *Paradise Lost*, then, Milton turns Horace's argument around. He does still juxtapose the themes of inspiration and celestial revolt, but just barely. They stand back to back, separated by the break between books, by the chasm between the poem's two halves. In the ode, on the other hand, they are more than juxtaposed, they are linked, albeit tenuously. The link, in fact, is extratextual: for Horace too is alluding to Hesiod's *Theogony*. Near the beginning of his poem, where the nine Muses are named for the first time in classical poetry, Hesiod says of Calliope: "She is foremost among all the Muses, for she attends upon reverent kings" (79–80). Throughout classical antiquity only Calliope was given such an individual concern; the association of each of the nine sisters with a proper discipline was largely a post-classical accomplishment. Horace accordingly names various other Muses in the *Odes* with apparent indifference.[35] But in 3.4, where he is preparing to advise his prince, the invocation of "regina . . . Calliope" recalls the Hesiodic context. (His extension of Calliope's association with rulers to the other Muses in lines 37–42 may be intended to aggrandize Caesar. There was nothing to prevent this synecdoche.) By alluding to Horace's ode, Milton relates the themes of inspiration and celestial revolt to one another, serving thereby not only the unity of his own poem but of his allusion to Hesiod. But by sundering the themes and reversing the order of their treatment, his allusion both emphasizes and rejects the crucial term that had permitted their conjunction in Horace's ode: the advising of the prince. And it is precisely this lacuna that is most significant for Milton.

To be sure, Milton's dismissal of Calliope is part of the antipagan bravado of *Paradise Lost*. But we should not be so ingenuous or so chauvinistic as to be persuaded by this religious enthymeme as if its premises were obvious and incontrovertible. On the one hand, Milton surely did not suppose that Christian poets were charmed or invulnerable: witness Edward King, whose drowning he also lays at Calliope's door. It is apparently the Muse's religion, not the poet's, that matters, and I am not sure what that can mean. On the other hand, a pretty good case can be made in Calliope's defense. No poet in antiquity regards Orpheus' death as evidence of Calliope's impotence.[36] And Horace is not the only poet whose experience testifies to the Muses' protection of their devotees. Among the others were Arion, Simonides, Ibycus, Archilochus, Aeschylus, Stesichorus, and Pindar—as Milton himself knew and recalled dramatically in Sonnet 8, titled "When the Assault was Intended to the City":

> Lift not thy spear against the muses' bower,
>   The great Emathian conqueror bid spare
>   The house of Pindarus, when temple and tower
> Went to the ground.
>
>   (9–12)

He styles his home the "muses' bower," meaning the classical Muses. Of course, this sonnet was written relatively early, when he still had the humanist's accommodating manners. By the time Milton came to write *Paradise Lost,* his allusive wit had become daring. He was willing to taunt, even to appear to slander the classics, as he does in the prologue to book 7. But we must always remember that he knew better. If we do not, we are Milton's fools, not God's. The larger point I am arguing is that his contention with the classics was a complicated affair. Milton's own position was ambivalent. His staged rejection of the classics is often a backhanded recommendation. And theology is not the only topic in dispute.

By politicizing his Muse, Horace politicizes himself. He is inspired by the civic Muse, at least in the Roman Odes. By rejecting Calliope, Milton implies his rejection of the restored King Charles II and simultaneously signifies his refusal of the classical poet's role as spokesperson on behalf of the civic community. Instead, he transfers the political virtues forfeited by king and community onto himself, by introducing a politically charged allusion to Orpheus, Calliope's son. Here he assimilates other texts to his allusion to Horace's ode. The tragic or elegiac aspect of the Orpheus myth is, of course, drawn from *Metamorphoses* 10 and 11. Ovid emphasizes Orpheus' failure to exert his prodigious poetic powers effectively in his own behalf. His song can animate rocks and trees, but fails to thwart his wife's mortality or his own.[37] But Milton is also drawing on an earlier, more positive view of Orpheus, known through the Renaissance from Horace's *Ars Poetica.* The picture there of the proto-poet as civilized and law-giver (391–401) harmonizes well with the Hesiodic (and now Horatian) association of Calliope with kings. These texts, so contrary in their connotations, are conflated in the prologue to book 7:

> drive far off the barbarous dissonance
> Of Bacchus and his revellers, the race
> Of that wild rout that tore the Thracian bard
> In Rhodope.
>
> (7.32–35)

If (as I believe) "Bacchus" refers to King Charles, whose carousing was notorious, these lines confess Milton's political despair.[38] Just as harmonious song connotes social order or *harmony* (as in "At a Solemn Music" or the angelic hymns that punctuate the days of Creation later in *Paradise Lost* 7), so "barbarous dissonance" here connotes anarchy or political *discord* as it had in the war in heaven in 6.667–68. The complex emotional truth in the charge that Milton urges against Calliope derives in part from his private self-identification with Orpheus and his disappointment at the vanity of his political career.

Milton's poetic interest in the story of Adam's fall long antedated the failure of the Cromwellian Protectorate. The events of 1660, however, did make possible, perhaps even compelled, a reading of Horace's ode that had never been available before. Milton was not the only poet to take advantage of it. Dryden, who had a much more Horatian temperament than Milton, recognized immediately the analogy between, on the one hand, England after the collapse of the Protectorate and Charles II's restoration, and, on the other, Rome after the demise of the Republic and Octavian's ascendance to unchallenged rule. Thus, addressing King Charles in 1660, Dryden concluded "*Astraea Redux:* A Poem on the Happy Restoration and Return of His Sacred Majesty Charles the Second":

> Oh Happy Age! Oh times like those alone
> By Fate reserv'd for Great *Augustus* Throne.
> When the joint growth of Armes and Arts foreshew
> The World a Monarch, and that Monarch *You.*

The implication in the word "foreshew" is that the relationship between Augustan Rome and Restoration England is virtually typological. What interests me particularly here is that, having drawn the historical analogy, Dryden proceeds to elaborate it in Horatian terms. He refers to the civil wars in terms of the gigantomachy, only emphasizing an element of the myth of which Horace had little need—the flight of the Olympians:

> Thus when the bold *Typhoeus* scal'd the Sky,
> And forc'd great Jove from his own Heaven to fly.
>
> . . . .
>
> The lesser Gods that shar'd his prosp'rous State
> All suffer'd in the Exil'd Thund'rers Fate.
>
> (37–38, 41–42)

Horace simply avers,

> magnum illa terrorem intulerat Ioui
> fidens iuuentus horrida bracchiis.
>
> (49–50)

(That gang of young toughs, confident, bristling with
arms, put great fear into Jupiter.)

Dryden's ultimate purpose in *Astraea Redux* is to plead for
clemency toward the defeated. Like Horace's Muse, he offers
"lene consilium":

> But you, whose goodness your discent doth show,
> Your Heav'nly Parentage and earthly too;
> By that same mildness which your Fathers Crown
> Before did ravish, shall secure your own.
> Not ty'd to rules of Policy, you find
> Revenge less sweet then a forgiving mind.
>
> (256–61)

Milton's allusion to Horace suggests the analogy, too, but only
to undercut it. The parallel between Charles and Caesar did
not serve his purpose.[39] Dryden's allusion simply adds another
level of historical allegory to the interpretation of the mythic
rebellions. Milton undercuts the myth and presents its arche-
type, the revolt of the bad angels. I think this is not just a
typologizing trick motivated by a desire to come in first in the
contest even though one started last. It betrays, rather, a desire
to quit the game altogether, to abandon the petty historical
one-upmanship.

My analysis would seem to leave us finally with the differences between these poets' interpretations of their personal
and political experiences. The differences are indeed pronounced and significant. Both poets began as republicans,
but they reacted quite differently to the failure of their original causes. Milton saw himself in heroic and ultimately tragic
terms, champion of a national cause until it abandoned him,
at which point he became a man outside and above politics.
William Kerrigan and others have observed, apropos of *Para-*

dise Lost's four great invocations, that Milton wished not only
to assume the role of the inspired prophet, but to remind his
readers of the noteworthy part that he himself had played in
the events of the previous two decades.[40] Horace, too, recalls
the part he played on the battlefield at Philippi, serving under
Brutus and Cassius, in *Odes* 3.4:

> uestris amicum fontibus et choris
> non me Philippis uersa acies retro,
> . . . extinxit.
>
> (25–27)

> (Friend to your fountains and choirs, I survived the rout
> at Philippi.)

Here in 3.4, though the tone is less than heroic, he is being
fairly serious because his military experience contributes to
the authority with which he addresses the subject of civil war.
But this line about Philippi looks back to an earlier poem, *Odes*
2.7, in which, speaking to a former comrade-in-arms, he recalls the defeat of the Republicans at greater length and more
intimately. This time he credits his escape to the less austere
patron Mercury and the mock-heroic expedient of a battlefield
cloud. And he accommodates his undignified and hasty retreat
to literary tradition by alluding to Archilochus' unapologetic
farewell to his shield.[41] Milton likewise draws upon literary
tradition to interpret his experience, but he chooses a heroic
myth instead, that of Bellerophon (*Paradise Lost* 7.17–20).

   Their different political conclusions are reflected most fundamentally in their different conceptions of themselves as
poets. J. H. Finley, whose 1937 article on Milton and Horace
focuses on the sonnets, found a deep affinity between the two
poets. Milton's sympathy for Horace, Finley says, was "largely

artistic and sprang from his recognition in Horace . . . of those conceptions of the power and importance of poetry which Milton shared"; and of Horace he observes, "no ancient poet, with the possible exception of Pindar, expressed more clearly the high purpose of the poet's calling."[42] Part of the problem here is that Finley confuses Milton the sonneteer with the blind seer of *Paradise Lost*. But more fundamentally, his argument mistakes Horace's playing of the vatic role by taking it at face value, in which it does resemble Milton's role. Commager has corrected this view for our benefit, exposing the ironic conventionality of Horace's vatic self-portrait and probing its anomalous depths.[43] Horace wore his bard's robes lightly. He was able to speak to his emperor and fellow citizens, becoming the equivalent of poet laureate in 17 B.C. when he was chosen to write the *Carmen Saeculare;* but he almost never speaks without irony. Milton risked everything for a political cause and lost; in the end he was not a poet laureate, but a prophet crying out to an apostate people. *The Ready and Easy Way to Establish a Free Commonwealth* was written only months before Dryden's *Astraea Redux,* but the contrast in tone is stark:

> What I have spoken, is the language of that which is not call'd amiss *the good Old Cause:* if it seem strange to any, it will not seem more strange, I hope, then convincing to backsliders. Thus much I should perhaps have said though I were sure I should have spoken only to trees and stones; and had none to cry to, but with the Prophet, *O earth, earth, earth!* to tell the very soil itself, what her perverse inhabitants are deaf to. Nay though what I have spoke, should happ'n (which Thou suffer not, who didst create mankind free; nor Thou next, who didst redeem us from being servants of men!) to be the last words of our expiring libertie.

But I trust I shall have spoken perswasion to abundance of
sensible and ingenuous men.   (*Complete Prose Works of John
Milton*, ed. Wolfe, 7:462–63)

One plainly discerns here a mind wavering between exalted
hope and plumb despair. Not long afterward this tension was
resolved, and the retired partisan turned poet-prophet addressed himself to "fit audience, though few."

The Playfulness of the Miltonic Critique

It would be premature to draw conclusions here—we have yet
to come to Vergil—but I do want to comment on the *duplicity*
of Milton's allusive strategy as observed so far.

First, each allusion—distinct as it is from the various lesser
connections between texts that we loosely designate *echo, borrowing, reminiscence*—consists of at least two terms, Hesiod's
line, for example, and Milton's, both of which stand in need
of full contextual interpretation. An allusion, in other words,
is a miniature hermeneutic dialogue. Which voice speaks first
is moot (Milton responds to Hesiod, but the response initiates
the dialogue); neither voice has the last word. Unfortunately,
most of Milton's twentieth-century exegetes have been willing, if not eager, to hear only one side of this poetic wrangle
and have prematurely declared Milton the winner. It has apparently troubled very few that this is egregiously unfair to
the classical poet, not to mention being quite inconsistent with
Milton's own principles, as far as we can determine them: "I
cannot praise a cloistered virtue, unexercised and unbreathed,
that never sallies out and sees her adversary" (*Areopagitica*).

But the word *dialogue* is inadequate, because the allusions
to Hesiod and Horace that I have been explicating are not
local effects, each standing on its own. Milton does not fin-

ish his conversation with Hesiod, hang up the telephone, and then ring Horace. Rather, the hermeneutic conversation that he initiates with one target text expands to include others, so that in the end the effect is like a multiparty conference call. The allusions to Hesiod and Horace work in concert, which is not at all the same thing as saying that Milton harmonizes the Roman with the Greek. But there are other voices to be heard as well. If we are patient, they will speak up when they are ready.

And what about the critique? I think it is a rhetorical ploy, designed to spark debate, not a philosophical or theological weapon designed to close debate off. Milton's key allusions to Hesiod appear to be deliberately *provocative*. But in itself this provocation is an incitement, not an indictment, and the act of reinterpretation is left to us readers. It is no doubt likely that John Milton the Puritan pamphleteer judged the *Theogony* to be theologically misinformed, and many scholars would see in this likelihood the end of the entire matter. But I think that would be to regard the literalism of the seventeenth century—or at least of Milton—simplistically, that is, *too* literally, and to convict Milton the poet of misunderstanding Hesiod's poetry in a way we ought to regard as quaint, if not downright silly. Milton brazenly contradicts Hesiod's text, but this is neither a conclusive victory, rendering the pagan poems obsolete, nor a "misprision" (as another theory might have it) due to Milton's or the seventeenth century's inability to perceive and accept Hesiod's meaning in its own terms. Recognition of the counterpoise provided by Horace is, I think, crucial if one is to avoid the simplemindedness of much of what has been written in this century about Milton's classicism.

The attitude toward the classics that one elaborates from *Paradise Lost* as a whole is at once profoundly ambivalent,

ironic, serious, and playful. I have not emphasized the play-
fulness, I admit, but it is there for those who can appreciate
it. Milton's strong allusions are in one respect a species of wit.
In this respect Milton may be Pope's greatest teacher, and
Horace may be one of Milton's.[44] The effect of this complexity
of attitude is to encourage us to reconsider the classics for ourselves, not, I think, in order to reject them, but in order to see
how they stand up to Milton's insolence. They do indeed stand
up. In other words, a thoughtful reading of Milton's allusions
(which is as good as to say a thoughtful reading of *Paradise Lost*)
should reinvigorate our understanding of the ancient poems
and their meaningfulness for us. That it seems to have done
this rather seldom in this century is not Milton's fault. We are
all of us busy people with better things to do than to take up
the study of dead languages.

3

Facilis descensus Auerno:
Design

Homer and Vergil

Prefixed to the second edition of *Paradise Lost* (1674), alongside the famous dedicatory English verses by Andrew Marvell, is a little-known Latin epigram by one Samuel Barrow, M.D. It begins:

> Qui legis Amissam Paradisum, grandia magni
> Carmina *Miltoni*, quid nisi cuncta legis? [1]

> (You who read *Paradise Lost*, the grand song of the great Milton, what is it that you are reading if not everything?)

He proceeds to illustrate the encylopedic comprehensiveness of Milton's poem; then he concludes by suggesting that Milton has left Homer and Vergil both in the dust:

> Cedite *Romani* scriptores, cedite *Graii*,
> Et quos fama recens vel celebravit anus.
> Haec quicunque leget tantum cecinisse putabit
> *Mæonidem* ranas, *Virgilium* culices.
>
> (39–42)

> (Give way, you Roman writers, give way, you Greeks,
> and also you whomever fame, whether recent or long-

standing, has honored. Whosoever reads this poem [viz.
Paradise Lost] will think that Maeonides [Homer] sang
only of frogs and Vergil, of mosquitoes.)

The final line refers to two of the *opera minora* then often
attributed to Homer and Vergil respectively, the mock epic
Batrachomyomachia ("Battle of Frogs and Mice") and the *Culex*
("Mosquito"), a neoteric delicacy. In the first of these four
lines, Barrow alludes to Propertius' famous anticipation of the
Aeneid while it was still a work-in-progress:

> Cedite Romani scriptores, cedite Graii:
>   nescioquid maius nascitur *Iliade*.
>
>   (2.34.65–66)

> (Give way, you Roman writers, give way, you Greeks:
>   something greater than the *Iliad* is being born.)

What is interesting is that, while Propertius refers to the *Iliad*
as the undisputed zenith of the epic tradition, Barrow cites
both Vergil and Homer, and, for that matter, nods at all the
other more or less recent contenders for the laurel crown, presumably including such worthies as Ovid, Dante, Tasso, and
Spenser.

In fact, it is not clear exactly how—or even whether—
Milton distinguished Homer from Vergil, either as exemplars
of epic practice or as targets of his attempted *coup de tradition*. The many volumes of Milton's prose and earlier poetry
provide surprisingly little insight into his opinions about his
two greatest classical predecessors. In one of his earliest references, he expresses a rather conventional opinion of Vergil's
superiority. Writing to Charles Diodati in his first *Elegy*, he
contrasts the pleasantness of his rustication from Cambridge
to Ovid's banishment to the Black Sea:

O utinam vates nunquam graviora tulisset
   Ille Tomitano flebilis exul agro,
Non tunc Ionio quicquam cessisset Homero,
   Neve foret victo laus tibi prima Maro.

(21–24)

(Would that the bard, a pitiable exile in the land of
Tomis, might never have suffered anything worse; then
he would not have been inferior in any way to Homer,
and having been conquered, you, Vergil, would no
longer hold the first honors.)

Of course, the hyperbolic praise of Ovid here undercuts even
the granting of honors to Vergil; and it should be remembered
that in his elegies Milton is chiefly apprenticed to Ovid.[2] Years
later in his *Defensio Prima* Milton described Vergil as "summus
artifex decori" (*Works of John Milton*, ed. Patterson, 7:324: "the
greatest craftsman of decorum"). This more interesting phrase
expresses a high estimation, considering Milton's remark in
Of Education that decorum is the "grand master peece to observe" (Wolfe, 2:405). Even so, it demonstrates only what
might in any case have been presumed, that Milton, despite
his extraordinary knowledge of Greek, was not unaffected by
the general prejudice of his age in regard to Vergil. Besides,
the remark is made in passing, at a moment when a boost to
Vergil's prestige is rhetorically useful. Further, decorum is not
the whole of poetry; and, praising Vergil is not necessarily the
same thing as dispraising Homer.

To my knowledge, nowhere else in his prose or poetic writings does Milton state a preference for one poet over another.[3]
Many claims have been made on this score by later critics.
Samuel Johnson reported, "The books in which his daughter,
who used to read to him represented him as most delighting,

after Homer, which he could almost repeat, were Ovid's *Meta-morphoses* and Euripides."[4] But the evidentiary value of this is slight. (Louis L. Martz even mentions a suggestion by one of his students apropos of this claim in Johnson, that Milton knew his Vergil by heart and had no need of a reader.[5]) I can find no evidence to support the suggestion of an estimable Miltonist, E. M. W. Tillyard, that the *Odyssey* was Milton's "favourite epic."[6] These are the impressions or fantasies of critics. But Milton himself says little or nothing to help us distinguish his view of Homer from his view of Vergil.

On the contrary, he frequently mentions the poets together and with the same tone, just as Barrow does in his dedicatory verses. In *The Reason of Church Government* he speaks of "that Epick form whereof the two poems of Homer, and those other two of Virgil and Tasso are a diffuse, and the Book of Job a brief model" (Wolfe, 1:813). The note on "The Verse" (added in the 1668 printing) states, "The measure is English Heroic verse without rhyme, as that of Homer in Greek, and of Virgil in Latin."[7] Similarly, in the invocation to book 9, lines 13–19, he couples Homer's epics with Vergil's, apparently to attack them equally.

There his comparison of his epic subject to those of Homer and Vergil is replete with sly innuendo. "I now must change / Those notes to tragic," he says, as he anticipates the action of his books 9 and 10:

> sad task, yet argument
> Not less but more heroic than the wrath
> Of stern Achilles on his foe pursued
> Thrice fugitive about Troy wall; or rage
> of Turnus for Lavinia disespoused.
> (9.13–17)

Wrath here is Homer's own word, μῆνις. Its position as the first word of the *Iliad*—Μῆνιν ἄειδε, θεά ("Wrath be your song, goddess")—was taken from Servius onward to be emblematic of the subject of the poem. Thus in the dedicatory essay to the Earl of Somerset prefixed to his translation of the *Odyssey*, George Chapman explains of Homer:

> And that your Lordship may in his face take view of his Mind, the first word of his *Iliads* is μῆνιν, wrath; the first word of his *Odysses*, ἄνδρα, Man—contracting in either word his each worke's Proposition.   (Nicoll, 2:4)[8]

Milton's reference to Turnus is likewise based on the original text. Milton's "rage" translates Vergil's "ira," Turnus' governing emotion. Vergil's "ira," in turn, plays against Homer's μῆνις. Vergil says of Turnus when we first see him, after he has been provoked by Allecto,

> arma amens fremit, arma toro tectisque requirit;
> saeuit amor ferri et scelerata insania belli,
> ira super.
>
>   (7.460–62)

> (Madly he bellows for arms, calls for arms from his bed-side and the halls. His love of the sword runs riot and with it the wicked insanity of war, and rage above all.)

Achilles' wrath is a complex thing that develops in stages throughout the poem, but it is aroused initially by the confiscation of his prize girl, Briseis, by Agamemnon. (Turnus' rage is simpler; it results from his loss of Lavinia to Aeneas and does not develop further.) But Milton does not mention or allude to Achilles' quarrel with Agamemnon over Briseis, and the grammar of these lines would lead a reader ignorant of the *Iliad* to suppose that Achilles' wrath was aroused by the "foe," i.e., Hector. But what we have here is a nice example of the enthymemic character of many of Milton's allusions that I mentioned in chapter 1. Milton was not writing for an audience ignorant of the *Iliad,* and he expects them to fill in for themselves the connection between "wrath," which alludes to the beginning of the *Iliad,* and "foe pursued," which alludes to the end. Milton thus leaves the entire *Iliad* to be read between the lines.

If the allusions to Achilles and Turnus, notwithstanding their subtlety, are based upon conventional interpretations and justified by specific reference to the poetic texts, the allusions to Ulysses and Aeneas appear to mistake seriously the actions of the *Odyssey* and the first half of the *Aeneid.* Indeed, the allusions are not to Odysseus and Aeneas at all:

> Or Neptune's ire or Juno's, that so long
> Perplexed the Greek and Cytherea's son.[9]
>
> (9.18–19)

"Ire" here parallels "wrath" and "rage" in the preceding lines. But this parallel is a sophistic sleight of hand. The syntax is not complicated, yet the absurdity of the meaning is easily missed because of the separation of the terms of the comparison. Milton is saying, "Sad task, yet argument not less but more heroic than . . . Neptune's and Juno's ire."

The point of this transumption of the first half of the *Aeneid* and the whole of the *Odyssey* under the heading of "wrath" and "ire" becomes clear in the following lines, when Milton says that he is

> Not sedulous by nature to indite
> Wars, hitherto the only argument
> Heroic deemed, chief mastery to dissect

With long and tedious havoc fabled knights
In battles feigned; the better fortitude
Of patience and heroic martyrdom
Unsung.

(9.27–33)

It becomes clear here that Milton acknowledges and takes to task only a single strain of classical heroism whose character he finds exemplified in the *Iliad* preeminently. But he does this by misrepresenting the plots and themes of the classical epics so egregiously that he can hardly have intended to fool anyone: a reader who does not object to the lines just quoted is not paying attention.[10] Milton's lens expands here to take in his more recent predecessors as well as the ancients, but the classical works to which he had referred just a few lines earlier are by no means exemplars of martial heroism exclusively, lines 28–29 to the contrary notwithstanding. Battle occupies a very small part of the *Odyssey*. The *Aeneid* has its battles ("dicam horrida bella," announces Vergil at 7.41), but they occupy only a third of the poem, and Vergil's own critique of the waste and futility of war is one of the most profound aspects of his poetic vision. Furthermore, "patience," in its Latin sense "endurance," is certainly characteristic of Aeneas and Odysseus both; and "heroic martyrdom" applies at least as well to Aeneas as to Adam. Odysseus' cleverness is easily made into a vice;[11] but, of course, his devotion to wife and home is not, and it would do Milton's argument no good to acknowledge it. It would have been even more inept to concede Aeneas' *pietas*. But these rhetorical considerations do not amount to a defense of Milton's misreading.

Alas, this is all a pretty abstract matter. John M. Steadman and others have made much of little, but Steadman in particular seems not to have taken into consideration that Milton may be capable of irony.[12] Milton's criticism of Homeric martial virtue is not supported with particular critical allusions of the sort that he uses to articulate his engagement with the Bible and the *Aeneid*. Most of those lines or phrases that have been recognized as possible allusions to Homer had already been echoed by Vergil. Milton's allusions to Homer, in other words, are seldom pure, that is, direct or unambiguous. The simile likening the legions of fallen angels to the "autumnal leaves that strew the brooks / In Vallombrosa" (1.302–3) recalls *Iliad* 6.146; but it also recalls *Aeneid* 6.309–10, not to mention Dante, *Inferno* 3.112–3, and Isaiah 34.4. The bee simile at *Paradise Lost* 1.768–75 can only be regarded as a weak reference to *Iliad* 2.87–90, considering the renown of Vergil's elaborations upon the Homeric original: a general one at *Georgics* 4.149–227 and a more specific one at *Aeneid* 1.430–36. The simile likening the legions of good angels to the birds flying over Eden recalls not only *Iliad* 2.459–63, but also *Aeneid* 7.699. Most of these compound allusions are similes, and the simile is the most conventional of the epic conventions.

There is one critical allusion to Homer in *Paradise Lost*. Satan, whom many critics have taken as the very embodiment of the Homeric "virtues" that Milton rejects, avers early in book 1:

> in my choice
> To reign is worth ambition though in hell:
> Better to reign in hell, than serve in heaven.
> (1.261–63)

Milton alludes to the dead Achilles' confession to Odysseus:

> βουλοίμην κ' ἐπάρουρος ἐὼν θητευέμεν ἄλλῳ,
> ἀνδρὶ παρ' ἀκλήρῳ, ᾧ μὴ βίοτος πολὺς εἴη,
> ἢ πᾶσιν νεκύεσσι καταφθιμένοισιν ἀνάσσειν.
> (*Odyssey* 11.489–91)[13]

(I would prefer to live as a serf in thrall to someone else,
    even a poor man without much of an estate, than be the
    ruler of all the perished dead.)

The allusion is marked as *critical,* in the sense that I have defined above, by the reversal of the terms of the target: Satan
aspires to that which Achilles rejects. Moreover, it satisfies
another of the criteria for importance that I have listed: it is
repeated. In book 6, Abdiel taunts Satan:

> Reign thou in hell thy kingdom, let me serve
> In heaven God ever blest.
>
> $$(183-85)$$

So Milton underscores the importance of his target, significantly, because the allusion demonstrates that the critique
of martial heroism ascribed to him by Milton's sycophants is
already found in Homer.[14] Milton seems to allude again to
these lines, or at least to the choice of Achilles, at 12.219–
20, where he implies that Israel was wise to avoid "inglori-
ous life with servitude," that is, precisely what Achilles, in
his belated wisdom, recommends in *Odyssey* 11. The apparent
contradiction may be resolved if one recalls the commonplace
distinction between ethical and political virtues.[15] For Milton,
servitude (that is, obedience) to God was, in fact, the greatest freedom, whereas political servitude was something to be
abhorred. Can we infer from this third occurrence of the allusion that Milton finds an objectionable confusion of ethical
and political virtues in Homer?

It is hard to say. Fowler, at 1.263, notes that Satan's sen-
timent or its contrary seems almost a commonplace, and he
cites half a dozen other instances of its expression. It ought
to make a difference whether the meaning of an allusive target is equivalent or contrary to the meaning of the alluding
text, but I cannot make out exactly what that difference might

be. Moreover, Fowler's list is not exhaustive. Hume applauds
Satan's bravado ("To Reign, though but in Hell, is desirable,
and worth attempting; Well exprest!"); then he cites Vergil
addressing Augustus at the opening of the *Georgics:*

> nam te nec sperant Tartara regem
> nec tibi regnandi ueniat tam dira cupido,
>
> (1.36–37)

> (Tartarus does not wish you for its king, and may such
> an extreme desire to rule never come to you.

He either did not notice the wholly contrary thrust of Vergil's
lines or did not feel that the inconsistency needed comment.

Homer himself is mentioned once in *Paradise Lost,* an honor
Vergil does not share.[16] In the proem to book 3, Milton places
Homer alongside Thamyris, Tiresias, and Phineus:

> nor sometimes forget
> Those other two equalled with me in fate,
> So were I equalled with them in renown,
> Blind Thamyris, and blind Maeonides,
> And Tiresias and Phineus prophets old.
>
> (3.32–36)

Thamyris, like Orpheus to whom Milton has alluded a few
lines earlier ("Orphean lyre," line 17), was a mythical poet
mentioned by Homer (*Iliad* 2.502–9) and said by Plutarch in
his treatise *On Music* to have written a poem on the titanomachy. Tiresias and Phineus were, of course, mythical seers
rather than poets. The former had been celebrated in Sopho-
cles' Oedipus plays and in Ovid's *Metamorphoses* 3, and the
latter in Apollonius' *Argonautica* 2. Of the four figures (five
if one counts Orpheus), only Homer may be thought of as
historical; and even if Milton's era might have been less sen-

sitive than ours to this distinction between the mythical and
the historical, it would have recognized that Homer was still
represented by his poetic productions in a way that the others
were not.

It is, of course, likely that Milton felt a personal affinity
with Homer by reason of their sharing both a talent and an
affliction; Milton here draws attention to the affliction ("blind
Maeonides"). But we cannot conclude from this that he is
aligning himself particularly with Homer. Quite apart from
the fact that Homer stands here in the midst of a crowd, there
is the fact that the figure of Vergil lurks just beneath the surface of the passage:

> Yet not the more
> Cease I to wander where the Muses haunt
> Clear spring, or shady grove, or sunny hill,
> Smit with the love of sacred song.
>
> (3.26–29)

The allusion to Vergil in the *Georgics,* in the most famous invocation in Latin literature, is unmistakable:

> Me uero primum dulces ante omnia Musae,
> quarum sacra fero ingenti percussus amore,
> accipiant caelique uias et sidera monstrent. . . .
>
> (*Georgics* 2.475–77)[17]

> (Indeed, first may the Muses, who are sweeter to me
> than anything, whose rites I perform, smitten with
> enormous love, accept me and show me the paths of
> heaven and the constellations.)

Both Milton's and Vergil's passages state the poet's commit-
ment to poetry in terms at once personal and quasi-philo-
sophical. Milton's association of himself with Vergil is not less

significant for being so discreet. I am left with the feeling that Homer's texts in Milton's allusions are called upon more for their prestige than their proper content. Even Dante, who had no direct knowledge of Homer's poetry whatever, salutes him in Limbo as "poeta sovrano."

"A Poem in Twelve Books"

The Romans taught the later West how to relate to its literary predecessors, which, of course, soon included the Romans themselves. Milton almost always sees Homer *through* Vergil, which is to say that Milton's Homer often looks pretty Vergilian. But in this Milton is not unique: it is true of almost every epic poet in the later tradition, so that one may even say that, after Vergil, writing epic largely meant imitating Homer in Vergil's manner.[18] There are detours or demurrals—in antiquity, the most successful is Ovid's *Metamorphoses;* the most important failure is Lucan's *Bellum Ciuile*—but, on the whole, Vergil's approach was paradigmatic.

Ironically, because imitation of Vergil was de rigueur, the most obviously Vergilian aspects of *Paradise Lost*—its literary allusiveness, elevated diction, and long verse paragraphs, and its division into twelve books—have been easy to dismiss as technical debts. The verse paragraphs, for example, do depend not just on the use of blank verse, but particularly on Milton's fondness for enjambment, which is Vergilian and not typically Homeric (nor, for that matter, particularly Ovidian); and few poets of epic handle this characteristic of Vergilian rhetoric as masterfully as Milton. But this sort of thing, while it may be noticed, does not cry out to be interpreted. It is apparently in this context that the division of *Paradise Lost* into the same number of books as Vergil's *Aeneid* has most often been considered. Milton seems to draw attention to the book divisions in the subtitle found on the title pages of early editions: "A Poem in Twelve Books," but this twelve-book structure has usually been taken as acknowledging Vergil's preeminence as the schoolmaster of epic poets, rather than suggesting any special purpose to the division of books. That the first (1667) edition of *Paradise Lost* was originally published not in twelve books, but in ten books, seems almost to confirm the arbitrariness of the Vergilian echo.

It seems worth noting that Milton's favorite English epics, Spenser's *Faerie Queene* and Abraham Cowley's *Davideis,* though both left unfinished, were both planned in twelve books. Cowley openly confesses the primacy of the Vergilian precedent in the preface to his *Poems* (1656). Spenser's motives were more complicated. He claims in his letter to Sir Walter Raleigh about the *Faerie Queene* that the twelve intended books are to reflect "the twelve private morall vertues, as Aristotle hath devised." But it appears that the virtues that Spenser purposed to treat were not precisely those of Aristotle, and it seems likely that Vergil's precedent influenced Spenser's decision, at least as strongly as Aristotle's analysis.

Now scholars have noted in Milton certain Vergilian subdivisions more detailed than those in Spenser or Cowley. For example, in the proem to book 7, Milton announces, "Half yet remains unsung, but narrower bound / Within the visible diurnal sphere" (line 21), calling to mind the renewed invocation at the beginning of *Aeneid* 7, "maior rerum mihi nascitur ordo, / maius opus moueo" (7.44–45: "A greater order of affairs arises before me: I now undertake a greater task"), which similarly marks the division of the poem into two grand halves. Furthermore, one can observe a tripartite structure in *Paradise Lost*'s twelve books that seems to reflect a similar structure in the *Aeneid*. Vergil's poem may easily be divided into three sections of four books each, focusing in turn on Dido, Aeneas, and Turnus. Similarly, *Paradise Lost* appears to possess three "movements" of four books each, turning upon the actions of Satan, the Son, and Man, respectively.[19] The first and third parts of *Paradise Lost* are tragic, like the corresponding parts of Vergil's epic, while the central portions of each poem are more hopeful.

But if this is all there is to it, a reader coming to Milton from Vergil is bound to be unimpressed. These few structural parallels are just elaborate enough to suggest that Milton is trying to play against Vergil, but so limited that they do little more than remind the reader of the imagination or ingenuity that Vergil has lavished on his parallels with Homer. What is most striking about Vergil's structural allusions to Homer is that they usually involve a degree of contradiction, reversal, reflection. For example, Vergil imitates the *Odyssey* in his first six books, and the *Iliad* in his second six, thus reversing the narrative order of Homer's poems. In his "odyssey," Aeneas is not going home to a waiting wife, but is leaving home, having lost his wife at the beginning. When he visits the underworld in book 6, Aeneas' prophetic guide is a woman, the sibyl, and he speaks to his father, Anchises; where in the *nekuia* of *Odyssey* 11, Odysseus consults with the male prophet Tiresias and then speaks to his mother. In the "iliadic" narrative, the Achillean figure, Turnus, robbed of the bride that he thought was his, fails to get her back and, indeed, ends up being defeated by the Hectorean figure of Aeneas.[20] And these are only a few of the most evident parallels.[21] This impulse to reversal is evident not only in aspects of the poem's design, but everywhere. For example, the *Aeneid*'s first simile (1.148–53) refers to the world of human action (the orator quieting a crowd) to illustrate an occurrence in the world of nature (the calming of

the tempest), which is a reversal of the usual Homeric relationship between tenor and vehicle.[22] Milton's mention of the
narrowing of his subject at 7.21 ("Half yet remains unsung,
but narrower bound") is a similar inversion of the expansion
claimed by Vergil ("maior opus moueo"), but it is more a verbal
than a structural reversal. In the end, the very superficiality
of Cowley and Spenser may seem less objectionable, like the
shallowness of the parallels between Joyce's *Ulysses* and the
Odyssey, because it raises no expectations.

Then again, perhaps we have been missing something in
Milton.

The Aeneid *Inside Out*

Odysseus' interview with Tiresias in *Odyssey* 11 is one of the
most mysteriously motivated parts of the poem. Odysseus
travels to the region of the dead and calls up the shade of
Tiresias because Circe had told him he would learn from
Tiresias the route home and the distance he would have to
travel (*Odyssey* 10.539–40). But the seer says nothing about
route and distance (11.100–37); in fact, he has little to say
about Odysseus' return home except to warn the hero not to let
his crew eat the cattle of the Sun. The rest of his remarks are a
combination of prophecy and advice about events *after* Odysseus has returned home, including the splendid anticipation
of Odysseus' death "from the sea." Odysseus and his mariners
return to Circe's island in book 12, and there he learns from
the witch herself the route and distance of his trip, in a long
and detailed speech (12.37–141). Moreover, her speech concludes with an emphatic and detailed warning about the cattle
of the Sun (127–41), which renders the briefer remarks of
Tiresias on this point superfluous. Of course, in spite of these
weak links with the narrative, *Odyssey* 11 is a book full of mar-

vels and contains material crucially important for the story in
other respects—in particular, the interviews with Achilles and
Agamemnon.

Vergil considerably expands the importance of Homer's
episode in his reworking of it in *Aeneid* 6. Aeneas' visit to the
underworld is acknowledged to be a spiritual lesson. There
is little pretense of practical benefit, but the lessons of the
visit are not rendered unnecessary by duplication elsewhere.
Helenus in book 3 simply advised Aeneas to consult the Sibyl
about the wars to be waged with the Italians (3.441–60), and
she does indeed address this subject, albeit somewhat crypti-
cally, in book 6 (83–97). The real business of book 6 is not
anticipated, however, until book 5, when the shade of Anchises
appears to Aeneas. Anchises says (724–37) that the Sibyl will
lead Aeneas through the realms of the dead to Elysium, where
father and son will meet again in person. Anchises will teach
Aeneas about the future of their race and about the city that
will be given to him ("tum genus omne tuum et quae dentur
moenia disces," 737). *Aeneid* 6 is the keystone of the poem's
structure and arguably its most important book. And its mys-
tic significance is enhanced by the fact that it draws not only
upon Homer, but upon two other grand precedents, the story
of Er in book 10 of Plato's *Republic* and, especially, the dream
of Scipio in the sixth book of the *Republic* of Cicero.

For Milton, the last and decisive exemplar is Dante's *Commedia*. Here there is no doubt but that the entire purpose of
the action is spiritual, and the descent is not a part of a larger
action, but is the entire action. Moreover, although the tidiness
of Dante's tripartite structure owes a great deal to the church's
doctrines regarding the assignment of souls after death to
Hell, Purgatory, or Heaven, nevertheless it answers to a similar structure in the descent of Aeneas, which also has three
parts. In the first or infernal part (*Aeneid* 6.295–547, not in-

cluding the vestibule of hell described in 268–94), Aeneas is
introduced to the grim conditions of the underworld. This
part anticipates much of Dante's and also Milton's infernal
decor. The second or Tartarean part of the descent (548–636)
is the briefest. As the Sibyl and Aeneas take a detour around
the place where the particularly wicked are punished, Aeneas
hears the groans and screams of the suffering souls (557–59),
and in response to his inquiry the Sibyl tells what she knows
from an earlier visit. Finally they come to the Elysian fields
(637), where Aeneas has his interview with Anchises, which
occupies most of the rest of the book (through 892). This section is almost exactly the same length as the first (256 lines
compared to 253 earlier). This third section is analogous to
Dante's Heaven, though the relationship of the other two sections to Dante's regions is somewhat less precise. (Vergil's first
section would seem to correspond to the *Inferno* less well than
his second, the excursus on punishments.) But the general
structure is unmistakably Vergilian.[23]

There are, of course, enormous differences between Dante's
very personal or "autobiographical" narrative and Milton's
more conventionally epic recounting of momentous events
from the distant past. But these poets have in common a perception of undeveloped potential in *Aeneid* 6, such as Vergil
himself had apparently seen in the *nekuia* of *Odyssey* 11. The
majority of *Paradise Lost*'s allusions to the *Aeneid* are directed
at the sixth book, not only in the first books of *Paradise Lost*,
but throughout the poem. Of larger consequence is the fact
that *Paradise Lost* is framed by parallels to *Aeneid* 6. The gist
of the design is this: the first two books of *Paradise Lost* correspond to the first or infernal part of the Vergilian descent,
and Milton's final two books correspond to the Elysian part of
the Aenean descent.

The first half of this structural homology is relatively easy to recognize. Satan and the fallen angels are, after all, in Hell, and much of the furniture is rented from Vergil. Milton's mention at 1.73–74 of the distance from Hell to Heaven, although the ratio is altered, recalls *Aeneid* 6.577–79 (compare with *Iliad* 8.16 and also *Theogony* 722–25). The "Stygian flood" (*Paradise Lost* 1.239) and "oblivious pool" (1.266) are details borrowed from Vergil's "Stygiam paludem" (6.323) and "Lethaei ad fluminis undam / securos latices et longa obliuia potant" (6.714). The gates of Milton's hell creak on their hinges as do those in Vergil's Hell (with *Paradise Lost* 2.879–82 compare *Aeneid* 6.573). Mention may also be made of the resemblance between the personifications seated with Chaos in Milton (2.959–67) and in Pluto's hall in Vergil (6.266–81). Two great similes support the connection. The first, comparing the dead to fallen leaves (*Paradise Lost* 1.302–4), has many other precedents besides the Vergilian one, but in this context the Vergilian pretext (*Aeneid* 6.309–10) is strongly felt.[24] More exclusively Vergilian is the hesitation in Milton's simile at 1.783–84 ("some belated peasant sees, / Or dreams he sees"), which is derived from Vergil's characterization of Aeneas' first uncertain recognition of Dido among the other shades ("aut uidet aut uidisse putat," 6.454: "he either sees or thinks he has seen").

Perhaps most significant of all the verbal links, because it is most peculiarly Vergilian, is Milton's allusion to Vergil's description of the difficulty of reascending from Hell to light:

> sate sanguine diuum,
> Tros Anchisiade, facilis descensus Auerno:
> noctes atque dies patet atri ianua Ditis;
> sed reuocare gradum superasque euadere ad auras,
> hoc opus, hic labor est.
>
> (6.125–29)[25]

(Son of Anchises, scion of Troy, bearer of the blood of
gods, the path down to Avernus is easy; night and day
the gate of gloomy Dis stands open. But to retrace your
steps to the upper air, to return: that's a task that takes
some doing.)

Thus the Sibyl warns Aeneas of the dangers of his ambition. In
Milton, the corresponding lines are spoken by Satan, to scare
off those that might wish to win easy glory by helping him:

O progeny of heaven, empyreal thrones,
With reason hath deep silence and demur
Seized us, though undismayed: long is the way
And hard, that out of hell leads up to light.

(2.430–33)

That the Vergilian lines occur in book 6 before the descent
begins is a matter of no consequence; I am not claiming that
Milton was always finicky about such details.[26] The import of
these lines is thematic, that is, they clearly call to the reader's
mind the epic precedent of Aeneas' descent.

The second, Elysian part of Aeneas' descent is paralleled in
the final two books of *Paradise Lost.* There has been some confusion over the precise epic precedent for Michael's prophecy
to Adam in *Paradise Lost* 11 and 12. The immediate source
of the episode was a similar episode in Du Bartas's *La Sept-
maine.*[27] But there is a crucial difference between immediate
source and authoritative precedent. After all, Du Bartas himself was following or reworking established conventions. Some
critics have taken the shield panoramas in *Iliad* 18 and *Aeneid* 8
as Milton's major epic precedents.[28] This is surely mistaken.
Achilles' shield is not prophetic, and even in *Aeneid* 8, the
ecphrastic mode of presentation is essential; but in the latter

books of Milton's poem we have a pageant, not an ecphrasis. The most significant parallel is patently with the pageant of heroes described to Aeneas by Anchises in the second part of the descent in *Aeneid* 6.[29] Michael performs a function analogous to that performed by Anchises. The key allusion is made at *Paradise Lost* 12.140, "Things by their names I call, though yet unnamed," which virtually translates *Aeneid* 6.776, "haec tum nomina erunt, nunc sunt sine nomine terrae."[30] Finally, if one imagines *Aeneid* 6 alone, instead of the entire poem, as at least in one way a primary structural model for *Paradise Lost* as a whole, then the length of the prophetic final books, about which many critics of Milton have complained, can be rationalized (if not poetically justified) on the ground of proportionality: the roughly 150 lines of Vergil's pageant constitute a sixth of the 901 lines of *Aeneid* 6, exactly the ratio of Milton's final two books to the total of twelve.[31]

The infernal and Elysian halves of Aeneas' descent are concerned with the past and the future, respectively. In the infernal part, Aeneas encounters figures from his past in reverse order, both of time and book: first Palinurus, from the end of book 5, the most recent dead; then Dido, from book 4; and finally Deiphobus, from the Trojan world whose ruin is related in book 2.[32] This encounter with the past is an ordeal of the spirit. Aeneas must come to grips with the pain of his past in order to meet the demands upon him that the future will make. The encounters in this part are closely modeled upon the interviews Odysseus has with Elpenor, Ajax, and Agamemnon in *Odyssey* 11. In this way, Vergil's encounter with his own poetic past in the person of Homer is an analogue of Aeneas' encounters with the figures from his past within the narrative. On the other hand, when Vergil turns to the prophetic narrative of Anchises, the substance of which is drawn from Roman history, he abandons his imitation of Homer. (It seems likely that Ennius became a more important model in Vergil's Elysian passage, with its references to generals from the Punic Wars and other early heroes, but in the absence of more of the *Annales,* it is impossible to guess at the extent of that importance.) The parallel between Anchises' prophecy and that of Tiresias is circumstantial, rather than personal or material. Indeed, Vergil takes pains to dissociate his vision of Roman history from the Greek world and its achievements (6.847–53: "excudent alii . . ."].

Milton's procedure is almost, but not quite, identical. The events in Hell in *Paradise Lost* 1 and 2, while not presented in a flashback or vision, do serve as background in relation to the crucial present in which Adam is awakening in Paradise. Moreover, Milton encounters his literary predecessors in these early books, just as Vergil had encountered Homer in his narration of Aeneas' infernal descent. Milton's Vergilian allusions and, indeed, his classical allusions, echoes, borrowings, and reminiscences generally are more abundant in the first two books of *Paradise Lost* than in the entire remaining ten.[33] On the other hand, books 11 and 12, which look forward to the future, are exceedingly sparing of classical allusions, for in these books Milton has turned to engage the Bible more openly than he does anywhere else. This sequence, from classical literature to Biblical, is a significant aspect of the progress of the poem's argument. But Milton's method differs from Vergil's in one crucial respect. Whereas the figure of Aeneas provided the continuity between past and future in Vergil's poem, there is no such personal continuity on the primary narrative level of *Paradise Lost.* Instead, the continuity between the classical past and the Biblical future depends on the figure of the poet himself.[34]

Milton as Aeneas? Not quite. Milton's use of the descent motif from *Aeneid* 6—with its Dantesque recommendation—is accomplished in a more complex manner. Drawing upon *Georgics* 4 and also books 10 and 11 of Ovid's *Metamorphoses,* Milton conflates the Aenean descent with the descent of Orpheus to the underworld in an attempt to recover his wife. The Orphean precedent is cited by Vergil. Aeneas says to the Sibyl that he is not the first hero to venture into the undergloom:

> potuit manis accersere coniugis Orpheus
> Threicia fretus cithara fidibusque canoris.
>
> (6.118–19)[35]

> (Orpheus was able to summon the spirit of his wife, relying only on his Thracian lyre and its tuneful strings.)

Note that Aeneas gives special emphasis to the musical or poetic prowess that Orpheus relied upon; this is particularly apposite to Milton's appeal to the precedent.[36] And Milton cites it himself in conjunction with the presentation of his own labors as a descent:

> With other notes than to the Orphean lyre
> I sung of Chaos and eternal Night,
> Taught by the heavenly Muse to venture down
> The dark descent, and up to reascend,
> Though hard and rare.
>
> (3.17–21)

The Miltonic descent is an Orphean, as well as an Aenean, move; the poet, in other words, is a hero. The Sibyl's warning to Aeneas—"facilis descensus Auerno," and the rest—occurs at 6.125–29, only a few lines after Aeneas mentions Orpheus, so it is not at all surprising to find Milton alluding here to both ideas in the proem to *Paradise Lost* 3. What is striking, though, is that Milton should allude to this passage a second time so soon after having used it in connection with Satan (2.430–33, see above).

The Aeneid *in a Mirror*

As I have suggested, the use of allusions to the sixth book of the *Aeneid* as a framing device for *Paradise Lost* suggests primarily a Dantesque design; it hardly makes the division of the poem into twelve books necessary. However, there is also a more distinctly Vergilian design woven into the structure of *Paradise Lost*, a pattern of detailed homologies based on a book-by-book inversion of the events of Vergil's poem. The *Aeneid* itself, by presenting Aeneas' "odyssey" before his "iliad," inverts the mythical chronology of Homer's epics. Milton's inversion is an example of the same process: certain books of *Paradise Lost* parallel the books of the *Aeneid* counted in reverse.[37]

The key to this pattern is provided by the two conciliar debates in *Paradise Lost*: the divine council of book 3 corresponds to the divine council of *Aeneid* 10 (third from the end), and the infernal council of *Paradise Lost* 2 corresponds to the council of the Italians (Aeneas' enemies in the war) in *Aeneid* 11 (second from the end). These parallels are simply structural, that is, they are not buttressed by an accumulation of verbal allusions.[38] In the case of the divine councils, this is no doubt due to Milton's sensitivity to the inappropriateness of exact comparison.[39] There are, however, some palpable points of similarity between the infernal council of book 2 and Vergil's Latin council. The topic being debated is the same in each (whether to fight or not); Moloch's bellicosity recalls that of Turnus; and

Belial, the coward with the golden tongue, resembles Vergil's orator, Drances.[40] I imagine that Milton regarded these parallels as fairly perspicuous; they do not, however, suggest any deeper points of contact between the poems. That is for the other parallels that readily suggest themselves, once the correspondence between the councils has been recognized. Let us turn first to *Paradise Lost* 4, the next in Milton's sequence; its attention to *Aeneid* 9 gives evidence that Milton's structural games, however little they may contribute to the poetry, are nevertheless informed by genuine critical intelligence.

Book 9 of the *Aeneid* recounts the siege of the Trojan camp by the Rutulians and Latins. Aeneas is absent from this book. (He is off seeking aid from Evander, the Etruscan king.) The two principal episodes of the book are the disastrous night raid of Nisus and Euryalus and the irruption of Turnus into the Trojan camp, where he wreaks havoc before escaping over the walls into the river. A significant aspect of the book's narration is Vergil's use of related similes throughout the book to characterize the progressive stages of the action. At the beginning of the book, on Aeneas' orders the Trojans have blockaded themselves in their camp, which Turnus is eager to assault. He is likened to a wolf, raging loudly outside a sheepfold late into the night, enduring harsh weather, maddened with hunger, while the lambs within bleat for their mothers (9.59–64). After the interlude of the night raid, the attack on the camp resumes and Turnus has his *aristeia*. At one point in the fighting before the ramparts, he snatches a certain Lycus, a Trojan, down from the wall as the latter attempts to escape. Here Turnus is likened first to an eagle, pouncing upon a hare or a swan (9.563–65), and then immediately to a wolf, now taking a lamb from its fold: "agnum / martius a stabulis rapuit lupus" (9.565–66: "the martial wolf took a lamb from its pen"). The double simile is emphatic. Near the end of the book, after the

Latins have invaded the camp and have been expelled, Pandarus manages to shut the unhinged gate against the enemy, failing to notice that he is shutting Turnus inside the camp with them. Here Turnus is likened to a huge tiger in the midst of the helpless herd (9.730). The change of animal vehicle here from wolf to tiger does not obscure the common circumstances of the several similes upon which the sense of development depends. The beast, at first repulsed, at last has access to his prey. At the very end of the book, when Turnus is about to be forced to leap the camp's walls to escape, he is compared to a fierce but frightened lion, beset by a crowd, unwilling to retreat, but unable to attack (9.792–96).

The action of *Paradise Lost* 4 subtly, but carefully, parallels the action of *Aeneid* 9. Satan is within the walls of Eden, despite the angelic guard. He threatens calamity, but is expelled forcibly before having accomplished his task. The parallel is marked by a critical allusion:

> As when a prowling wolf,
> Whom hunger drives to seek new haunt for prey,
> Watching where shepherds pen their flocks at eve
> In hurdled cotes amid the field secure,
> Leaps o'er the fence with ease into the fold:
> Or as a thief bent to unhoard the cash
> Of some rich burgher, whose substantial doors,
> Cross-barred and bolted fast, fear no assault,
> In at the window climbs, or o'er the tiles;
> So clomb this first grand thief into God's fold:
> So since into his church lewd hirelings climb.
>
> (4.183–93)

Behind the first part (183–87) of this grand double simile lie Vergil's two wolf similes and perhaps the one-line tiger simile as well.[41] Milton's simile lacks the emotional or psychological

intensity that makes Vergil's similes so chilling. Moreover, the
second image in Milton's double simile, of the burglar climb-
ing through a window, seems delicately droll in a most un-
Vergilian manner. Milton does make a splendid move here,
however, by conflating the vehicles of the two similes in line
192 ("So clomb this first grand thief into God's fold"), and
the concluding line ("So since into his church lewd hirelings
climb") vents a little impertinent Miltonic ire (compare with
Lycidas 113–15). To return to the allusion to Vergil, it suggests
not only a similarity in the general circumstances of *Paradise
Lost* 4 and *Aeneid* 9, but also implies a contrast between Turnus'
laborious attack and Satan's effortless trespass.

It may also be that Milton is alluding to, or at least drawing upon, the later succession of similes in *Aeneid* 9 likening Turnus to a tiger and a lion, in the metamorphoses that
Satan undergoes as he observes Adam and Eve closely for the
first time:

> about them round
> A lion now he stalks with fiery glare,
> Then as a tiger.
>
> (4.401–3)

With the "fiery glare" of Milton's line, compare Vergil's description of his lion, "acerba tuens" (9.794: "staring bitterly").
But Milton deflates all the natural nobility of these animal similes when he costumes Satan climactically as a toad, squatting
at the sleeping Eve's ear (4.800). Finally, there is more than
a little resemblance between the final simile of *Aeneid* 9 (the
cornered lion) and the final animal simile of *Paradise Lost* 4,
where Satan is compared to a curbed horse:

> The fiend replied not, overcome with rage;
> But like a proud steed reined, went haughty on,

Champing his iron curb: to strive or fly
He held it vain.

(4.857–60)

Here is Vergil's simile in full, with a bit of the narration before
and after:

acrius hoc Teucri clamore incumbere magno
et glomerare manum, ceu saeuum turba leonem
cum telis premit infensis; et territus ille,
asper, acerba tuens, retro redit et neque terga
ira dirae aut uirtus patitur, nec tendere contra
ille quidem hoc cupiens potis est per tela uirosque.
haud aliter retro dubius uestigia Turnus
improperata refert et mens exaestuat ira.

(9.791–98)

(Now more keenly the Trojans swell their ranks and
press upon [Turnus] with a great din, as a band of
hunters threatens a fierce lion with their weapons. The
frightened lion, violent, staring bitterly, retreats, but
neither its rage nor its courage let it turn its back, and
yet neither is it able, although it wants, to charge forward through the men and weapons. Not otherwise
does Turnus, uncertain, inch his steps backward, while
his heart boils over with rage.)

"To strive or fly" describes precisely the alternatives elaborated in Vergil's simile, and "overcome with rage" is a plausible
echo of "mens exaestuat ira." Certain differences between the
similes may be accounted for by the different events: Turnus,
after all, escapes, while Satan is taken captive. Nevertheless,
while the vehicles of these two similes are quite different, the

tenors are strikingly similar. This is typical of what I would describe as Milton's *translations* of Vergil: he is able to engage similar concerns through the telling of a superficially dissimilar story.

The only piece of the pattern of inversion left to be described is the parallel between Dido and Aeneas in *Aeneid* 4, and Eve and Adam in *Paradise Lost* 9 (the fourth book from the end). This is perhaps the most obvious natural correspondence between these two epics, whose stories otherwise have apparently very little in common.[42] *Aeneid* 4 belongs to Dido as clearly as *Paradise Lost* 9 belongs to Eve. But in the larger perspective, the importance of each book consists in the dilemma that it presents to the male heroes, Aeneas and Adam. In each case that crisis takes the form of a choice between love of a woman and obedience to divine will. In each case, the woman is led into error by a disguised immortal (Cupid posing as Ascanius, Satan as the serpent). The woman errs, then attempts to draw the man after her. The poet's attitude toward womankind in each case is ambivalent.

The foundation of the book parallel is a link made between Eve and Dido by means of a strong allusion. After having obtained Adam's reluctant permission to withdraw to do her work alone, Eve, departing, is likened to Diana (Delia):

> from her husband's hand her hand
> Soft she withdrew, and like a wood-nymph light
> Oread or dryad, or of Delia's train,
> Betook her to the groves, but Delia's self
> In gait surpassed and goddess-like deport,
> Though not as she with bow and quiver armed,
> But with such gardening tools as art yet rude,
> Guiltless of fire had formed, or angels brought.
>
> (9.385–92)

The first appearance of Dido in Aeneid 1 is similarly described
by comparison with Diana:

> qualis in Eurotae ripis aut per iuga Cynthi
> exercet Diana choros, quam mille secutae
> hinc atque hinc glomerantur Oreades: illa pharetram
> fert humero gradiensque deas supereminet omnis.
>
> (1.498–501)[43]

(Just so, on Eurotas' banks or Cynthus' ridges, Diana
leads her chorus, followed by a thousand Oreads crowd-
ing together on every side. She carries her quiver on
her shoulder and, stepping along, surpasses those god-
desses.)

Dido, too, is on her way to work, although her labors involve
giving laws, judging disputes, and apportioning building as-
signments, while Eve has only to prune the flowers. The points
of similarity that prove the allusion are numerous: Diana and
her chorus ("train"), the Oreads, the quiver, and, most con-
clusively, the exact reproduction of "gradiens supereminet"
as "in gait surpassed." What must be noticed, however, is the
care with which Milton has reworked the simile. In Vergil, it is
Diana to whom Dido is compared; it is her attendants that she
"surpasses." ("Supereminet" literally suggests that Diana was
taller than her attendants.) In Milton's simile, Eve is humbly
likened to one of the Oreads, not to the goddess herself; and
yet it is the goddess that she surpasses. As we have seen before, this sort of reversal of terms is the mark of Milton's critical allusions. Another incidental allusion linking Eve to Dido
may be intended in Adam's description of Eve as "to death
devote" (9.901), with which compare Vergil's description of
Dido, "pesti deuota futurae" (1.712: "marked out for coming
destruction").[44]

Dido enters the narrative at the end of *Aeneid* 1 (to which
these allusions are directed), and her tragedy is there fore-
shadowed. But it is book 4 that one thinks of as hers; she is the
center of attention throughout. (She is absent during Aeneas'
account of Troy's fall and his wanderings in books 2 and 3.)
Her story may be divided into three parts. In the first, "be-
guiled" (as Milton says of Eve) by Cupid, Dido responds to
Aeneas' charm and is tempted to break her vow of chastity
made upon her husband's death. This occupies roughly the
last hundred lines of book 1 and the first fifty of book 4. In
the second part, she has succumbed to her passion for Aeneas
and he (apparently) has not rebuffed her. They rule Carthage
jointly, and he assists in directing the construction of the city,
temporarily oblivious of his vocation in Italy. This occupies
roughly the next hundred and fifty lines of book 4. In the
third part, after learning that Aeneas is leaving, Dido is en-
raged and distraught; this part culminates in her suicide. This
occupies the remainder of book 4, roughly five hundred lines.

These three stages parallel three stages of the fall of Adam
and Eve: first, Eve's temptation and fall; secondly, Adam's
fall and their "amorous play" (9.1045); and, finally, recognition and remorse. Milton's allusion to Dido as Diana occurs
just as Eve is departing Adam on her chores; this begins the
first stage, her temptation. The next major allusion to the Dido
story occurs just after Eve has eaten the apple:

> So saying, her rash hand in evil hour
> Forth reaching to the fruit, she plucked, she ate:
> Earth felt the wound, and nature from her seat
> Sighing through all her works gave signs of woe,
> That all was lost.
>
> (9.780–84)

This response of Nature to sin is reiterated after Adam's fall (9.1000–3), making this an emphatic double allusion. The "fall" of Dido is her tryst with Aeneas in the cave during the thunderstorm that interrupted their hunt. Vergil modestly refrains from stating what takes place within the cave, but the response of Earth, Juno, Sky, and the Nymphs is appropriate to a wedding:

> speluncam Dido dux et Troianus eandem
> deueniunt. prima et Tellus et pronuba Iuno
> dant signum; fulsere ignes et conscius aether
> conubiis summoque ulularunt uertice Nymphae,
> ille dies primus leti primusque malorum
> causa fuit.
>
> (4.165–70)

> (Dido, the leader, and the Trojan came to the same cave.
> Earth first and bridesmaid Juno gave the sign. Light-
> ning and the knowing sky flashed at the nuptials, and
> nymphs howled on the mountain summit. That was
> destruction's inaugural day and the cause of evils.)

The interpretation of this ambiguous passage requires that we look before and after it. A little earlier, Vergil had shown the queen holding up the hunting party as she lingered in her wedding chamber in the palace ("thalamo cunctantem," 133). And a little later, Aeneas protests—perhaps a bit technically—that he never considered them married (338–39). Vergil's image of "pronuba Iuno" thus is characteristically terrifying. Juno, after all, is supposed to be Dido's patroness.

Both Vergil's and Milton's lines emphasize the phenomenal response of an animate nature.[45] Earth ("Tellus") is common to the two passages. Vergil's mention of lightning and

the sky lies vaguely behind Milton's reference to Nature at
9.782 and contributes more directly to 9.1002–3 (after Adam's
fall), "Sky loured, and muttering thunder, some sad drops
/ Wept." Milton's "gave signs of woe" translates and expands
"dant signum." Both passages conclude with interpretations
of the meaning of the phenomena: "all was lost," and "ille dies
primus leti." Of course, the larger contextual resemblances between these passages contribute to the appropriateness of the
allusion. It should surprise no one that Milton does not refer
to Juno or the nymphs.[46]

The final important link between *Aeneid* 4 and *Paradise
Lost* 9 consists of a pair of subtle, but closely related, allusions.
The link hinges on the simple word "certain," which Milton
uses twice in its Latinate sense, meaning "resolved" or "determined." Both uses occur in Adam's speech responding to Eve's
announcement that she has eaten the apple (9.896–959), one
near the beginning of the speech and the other near its close.
Near the beginning of his speech Adam reassures Eve:

> for with thee
> Certain my resolution is to die.
> (9.906–7)

The referent of this allusion is the description of Dido as
"certa mori" (4.564: "resolved to die"). I will come to the
association of Adam with Dido rather than Aeneas presently.
Let us notice first that later in the same speech, after having
meditated upon the dire consequences of Eve's crime, Adam
reassures her again:

> However I with thee have fixed my lot,
> Certain to undergo like doom.
> (9.952–53)

This should not perhaps be called an allusion in itself, for it translates less precisely than the previous example the Latin to which I would refer it, the words that characterize Aeneas' determination to leave Carthage, "certus eundi" (4.554: "resolved to go"). It is, however, a purer instance of the Latinism.[47] Moreover, Milton's use of the Latinism twice in the same speech is modeled on a similar repetition in Vergil. Vergil's two uses of the word occur exactly ten lines apart. Milton's two uses of "certain" occur a full forty-five lines apart but within the same speech and in positions of rhetorical emphasis. He was impressed with Vergil's repetition and imitated it.

Now, to return to the association of Adam with Dido in the first allusion ("certain . . . to die"). The single most obvious difficulty faced by Milton in his effort to pit Adam's crypto-Christian heroism against the pagan heroism of Aeneas was that Adam, in spite of quite explicit warnings and a full consciousness of the fact that he was sinning, had in the end succumbed to temptation, while Aeneas, in a moral situation much more ambiguous to begin with, had resisted temptation or at least had extracted himself from it before his irresponsibility had consequences fatal to his mission. In Milton's own terms, it appears that the classical hero could have successfully passed the test that the Biblical hero failed so spectacularly. By linking Adam with Dido, who was truly guilty of impiety, Milton stresses Adam's transgression and failure. However, the reworking of Vergil's "certus eundi" as "certain to undergo," by drawing attention to the difference between *going* and *undergoing,* suggests the positive quality of Adam's humanity. The "better fortitude / Of patience" (9.31–32) refers to the willingness to suffer—"patience" is a Latinism, from *patior,* "suffer"—rather than a willingness to wait. "Undergo" in its negative aspect implies the suffering that lies

ahead for Adam and Eve. In its positive aspect, however, by
suggesting subtly a certain latent nobility in Adam's resolution,
it hints at the paradox of good in evil that is ultimately the
foundation of an understanding of Redemption. The grand-
est aspects of Milton's vision can often be found thus implied
in the smallest details.

"*. . . imperium Oceano, famam qui terminet astris . . .*"

Milton was, of course, a republican, not a monarchist. He had
strong opinions about the events of the first century B.C., and
his sympathies were on the whole with such defenders of the
Republic as Cicero and Brutus:

> The Greeks and Romans, as thir prime Authors witness,
> held it not onely lawfull, but a glorious and Heroic deed,
> rewarded publicly with Statues and Garlands, to kill an in-
> famous Tyrant at any time without tryal. (*The Tenure of
> Kings and Magistrates;* Wolfe, 3:212)

Actually, Milton's attitude toward the assassination of Julius
Caesar seems to have been ambivalent. He believed that those
nations who succumbed to tyranny deserved it, and he criticizes Brutus and Cassius for not recognizing that "the nation
was not fit to be free."[48] It is a rather Tacitean view. (Tacitus
has the emperor Tiberius leaving the senate house muttering cynically to himself, "o homines ad seruitutem paratos!"
[*Annales* 3.65: "Men fit to be slaves!"]) Moreover, Milton appears to have considered Augustus a benevolent ruler and to
have regarded his monarchy as tolerant. In *Areopagitica,* he
defends Augustus in the cases of Livy and Ovid:

> And for matters of State, the story of Titus Livius, though
> it extoll'd that part which Pompey held, was not therefore

supprest by Octavius Caesar of the other Faction. But that
Naso was by him banisht in his old age, for the wanton
Poems of his youth, was but a mere covert of State over some
secret cause: and besides, the Books were neither banisht
nor call'd in.   (Wolfe, 2:499)

Then he remarks, "From hence we shall meet with little
else but tyranny in the Roman Empire" (Wolfe, 2:499–500).
Despite the mild attitude toward Augustus implied here, we
must stress the fundamental fact that Milton, like Tacitus,
considered Augustus, too, to have been one of "those Pagan
Caesars that deifi'd themselves" (Wolfe, 3:204). Tacitus expresses the transition of power from Augustus to Tiberius
with undisguised sarcasm: "sepultura more perfecta templum
et caelestes religiones decernuntur. uersae inde ad Tiberium
preces" (*Annales* 1.10–11: "After the customary funeral, Augustus was voted a temple and a god's cult-apparatus. Then
everybody's prayers turned to Tiberius"). Such extra-poetic
evidence as there is would lead us to expect that Milton's quarrel with Vergil would not have concerned the political qualities
of the historical Augustus, but would rather have concerned
the eschatological focus of Vergil's political religion. Vergil was
not wrong to praise Augustus as a good ruler. He was mortally
wrong, however, to consider Augustus as virtually the Roman
Messiah.

Paradise Lost's engagement of the *Aeneid*'s political dimension is concentrated in the analogy between Milton's Son and
Vergil's Augustus, which will suggest itself fairly readily, once
all the more detailed sorts of links between the two poems
have been recognized. There is, however, a verbal link here,
too. Michael concludes his prophecy in book 12 by describing
Christ's birth and his work as Savior:

> he shall ascend
> The throne hereditary, and bound his reign
> With earth's wide bounds, his glory with the heavens.
>
> (12.369–71)

The allusion is to a few lines in the prophecy given by Jupiter in *Aeneid* 1:

> nascetur pulchra Troianus origine Caesar,
> imperium Oceano, famam qui terminet astris,
> Iulius, a magno demissum nomen Iulo.
>
> (1.286–88)

> (From a beautiful source will be born Trojan Caesar,
> whose rule will be bounded by the Ocean and whose
> renown, by the stars: Julius, a name come down to him
> from great Iulus.)

I agree with R. D. Williams and others that Vergil is here refer-ring to Augustus rather than Julius Caesar, as Servius thinks.[49] The dramatic propriety of the context calls for a reference to the restorer of the Golden Age himself. Milton's allusion suggests that he interpreted the lines in this way, and part of the allusion's point, as I see it, depends on this. For I take Milton's allusion to be attempting to point up the shallowness of Vergil's great claims for Augustus by contrasting them with their application to the Son of God, in which connection they are uniquely valid.

But—as I asked at the beginning of the second chapter—can we take this critique very seriously? On the face of it, Milton appears to be censuring the confidence of Vergil's historical vision in a secular (and mortal) foundation. This criticism must seem to us absurd, though, since recent re-considerations of the *Aeneid* have rendered easily audible the

intentionally hollow ring of such passages.⁵⁰ The error of
Milton's critique would seem to have been caused by the
combination of his conventionally black-and-white reading of
the *Aeneid* with his own somewhat unconventional confidence
about the security of the universe's divine foundations. If we
travel this path, we are bound to conclude that one poem or
the other is radically mistaken about the disposition of Providence toward human affairs, or at least, in a desperate effort
to keep both poems, we will attempt to keep them safely separated, like church and state.

On the other hand, the initial explanation of the allusion
may have been too facile. Perhaps we *can* take this allusion
seriously, but if so, we must reconsider both poems. We need
not assume, because of a lack of historical evidence to the contrary, that Milton was insensitive to the ambivalence of Vergil's
vision. Indeed, we need only recall the ambivalence of his
own. It was not Vergil whom Blake claimed was "of the Devil's
party without knowing it" (*The Marriage of Heaven and Hell,*
plates 5–6). If we pursue Milton's reference to the *Aeneid* with
a lively sense of the tensions inherent in *Paradise Lost* we will
find ourselves not misdirected, but actually better attuned to
the tensions in the *Aeneid*. Of course, what we do with them
then is not for critics or poets to say.

"Tantaene animis caelestibus irae?"

When Eve hesitates to eat the fruit of the tree of knowledge,
the Serpent asks,

> What can your knowledge hurt him, or this tree
> Impart against his will if all be his?
> Or is it envy, and can envy dwell
> In heavenly breasts?
>
> (9.727–30)

The dramatic irony of the lines is obvious. While Satan may be unaware of it, his is certainly a "heavenly breast" in which envy dwells. Less obvious, but more significant, is what might be called the *epic irony*, arising from the fact that Milton is alluding to Vergil's question, "tantaene animis caelestibus irae?" (1.11: "Is there so much anger in heavenly minds?"), a question that might be taken to strike the keynote of the entire *Aeneid*. This is Milton's most important allusion to Vergil. The rhetorical effect of Vergil's question, placed so prominently in his proem, is analogous to the effect of Milton's ambitious line, "And justify the ways of God to men," which is similarly situated: each sentence reveals its poet's main concern. But the resemblance of the two lines is deeper than a coincidence of rhetorical purpose. Both lines seem fundamentally to be hinting at the same philosophical or religious problem, the impact of sin or evil or divine "ire" upon human experience. Even Milton's confident declaration implies that God's ways are in need of justification, perhaps even that to supply this justification is a bold and difficult labor. And yet the simple grammatical difference between the manner in which each poet announces his theme is pregnant with the difference between them. Vergil, who is not writing a theodicy, approaches this ontological and ethical uncertainty by means of a question, while Milton employs a declaration.

Near the end of his poem, Vergil asks a series of questions that recall those with which he had begun; they constitute a sort of negative invocation:

> Quis mihi nunc tot acerba deus, quis carmine caedes
> diuersas obitumque ducum, quos aequore toto
> inque uicem nunc Turnus agit, nunc Troius heros,
> expediat? tanton placuit concurrere motu,
> Iuppiter, aeterna gentis in pace futuras?
>
> (12.500–4)

(What god will now unravel for me so many bitter happenings? Who will unravel in song the various slaugh-
ters, the downfall of leaders that one after another,
now Turnus, now the Trojan hero, drives along the
shore? Did it please you, Jupiter, to crash together with
such confusion these races that one day would live in
lasting peace?)

These questions are plaintive. "What god will now unravel
for me so many bitter happenings?" The rhetorical effects are
typically masterful, and here we can see some of what Milton
(and the Western poetic tradition) learned from Vergil. The
collocation of words whose associations are incompatible is an
effective means of building tension: "acerba deus," "carmine
caedes" (emphasized by alliteration). The collocation of "quis
mihi"—very Latin, a very common device in Horace and elsewhere—here heightens the sense of distance between the poet
and the gods. There may be even a hint of accusation: what
god will give an account *to me?* All this dissonance builds, only
to be exploded in the innocent, but strategically placed, "expe-
diat." The word calls for the solution of a problem ("unravel,"
literally "loosen the feet" or "remove an obstacle from before
the feet"). The direct apostrophe to Jupiter in the last two of
the lines quoted brings Vergil's concern to its point.

His question here is unanswered. But not long afterward, in
the penultimate scene in the poem, Jupiter and Juno negotiate
a cessation of hostilities between themselves, and here both this
question to Jupiter and the opening question of the poem—
"tantaene animis caelestibus irae?"—are answered. The contrast between the pleasant tone of Jupiter's badinage with Juno
and the gravity of the subject of their conversation in terms
of human suffering is stark and chilling. Juno surrenders, but
by no means unconditionally. When she has stated her request
that the Latin name and language be preserved at the expense

of the Trojan (peculiarly linguistic concerns, these), Jupiter responds:

> olli subridens hominum rerumque repertor:
> "es germana Iouis Saturnique altera proles,
> irarum tantos uoluis sub pectore fluctus."
>
> (12.829–31)

> (Smiling at her, the ruler of men and matter says, "You
> are indeed Jupiter's twin, another offspring of Saturn,
> such torrents of wrath you turn in your heart!")

This last line answers Vergil's initial question almost word for word: "tantaene animis caelestibus irae?" Yes, "irarum tantos . . . fluctus." Note the emphatic placement of the final word.[51]

Juno was the instigator of all the woes that have beset Aeneas since he set sail from Troy. Throughout the poem we are led to sense a tension between Juno's wrath and Jupiter's unalterable design for the Trojans, a conflict which both assigns blame and reassures the reader of the outcome. Even when Vergil asks, "Did it please you, Jupiter, to crash together with such confusion these races?" (12.503–4, quoted above), one feels capable of saying, No, it was Juno's fault. But in the scene in heaven that follows, we witness Jupiter smiling at his consort, confessing her as his twin ("germana"), and announcing himself conquered by her: "do quod uis, et me uictusque uolensque remitto" (12.833: "I grant what you wish and resign myself, conquered and yet willing"). Mercifully we find a hint of irony here that saves this passage from being totally disheartening. The lines are shocking nevertheless. We had hoped for some illumination in answer to the thematic question at 1.11, and for a moment in book 12 we think we have it, when the "torrents of such great wrath" are revealed in Juno. But in the end it turns out that we know less about the gods than we had thought, especially Jupiter, "hominumque rerumque repertor."

This scanning of the first and final lines of the *Aeneid* hopes to imply the presence of a middle term. Vergil's question is not called up again when suddenly at 12.831 it is answered. It reverberates throughout the intervening twelve books of the poem. I submit that our response to the entire *Aeneid* is called into play by Milton's simple allusion: "Or is it envy, and can envy dwell / In heavenly breasts?" It is a challenging allusion. It was one thing to enhance Satan's character in the first two books by comparing him with Aeneas.[52] Then Milton knew he would have time to correct the false association. But here he associates Satan not with Aeneas, but with Vergil himself. Vergil, after all, had not intended to justify God's ways to men. He called them into question in the very act of persuading men to resign themselves to them. This questioning of God appears now to be relegated to the Serpent.

But the allusion is less simple than that. Milton's important allusions do not usually stand alone. I have already noted three "compound" or reiterated allusions to the *Aeneid: Paradise Lost* 2.430–33 and 3.20–21 to *Aeneid* 6.125–29 ("facilis descensus Auerno"); *Paradise Lost* 9.780–84 and 9.1000–3 to *Aeneid* 4.165–70 (the response of Nature to Dido's adultery); and the paired allusions, at *Paradise Lost* 9.907 to *Aeneid* 4.564 ("certa mori") and at *Paradise Lost* 9.953 to *Aeneid* 4.554 ("certus eundi"). "Tantaene animis caelestibus irae?" is so important to Milton—no doubt because it was so important to Vergil —that he refers to it not twice, but actually three times. The first is brief and easily missed. In book 4, Milton describes the tantrum that gives Satan away:

> Thus while he spake, each passion dimmed his face
> Thrice changed with pale, ire, envy, and despair,

> Which marred his borrowed visage, and betrayed
> Him counterfeit, if any eye beheld.
> For heavenly minds from such distempers foul
> Are ever clear.
>
> (4.114–19)

Thus the narrator himself avers. But at 6.788 we find, "In heavenly spirits could such perverseness dwell?" This is *Raphael's* question, not Satan's and not the narrator's, and the "heavenly spirits" are the bad angels. Raphael proceeds to describe them as "proud" and "obdurate" and says they "took envy" at the sight of the Son's exaltation (793). Envy, then, is precisely the consuming vice of the fallen angels and especially of Satan.[53]

In book 6 Milton's question is closely appropriate to the context of Vergil's opening. Each question is concerned with the mystery of the suprahuman origin of evil. Still, there are two differences between Vergil's question and that of Milton. Vergil's "animis caelestibus" refers to the very queen of the gods and thus strikes deeper to the heart of the divine order. Milton's question refers only to the bad angels. (I suppose that the first of Milton's allusions to *Aeneid* 1.11, the one in book 4 in which the narrator states firmly that such distempers are not found in heavenly breasts, is intended precisely to discourage the kind of questioning that Vergil encourages. This, at least, is not an instance of Fishian technique.[54]) Secondly, and this is more important, Vergil's question is genuine, whereas Milton's is at least partly rhetorical. Vergil's question concludes the opening paragraph of the poem and is left unanswered until *Aeneid* 12.831, at the end of the poem. Milton's question is countered immediately by another and then by a conclusive explanation:

In heavenly spirits could such perverseness dwell?
But to convince the proud what signs avail,
Or wonders move the obdurate to relent?
They hardened more by what might most reclaim,
Grieving to see his glory, at the sight
Took envy.

(6.788–93)

It should not be supposed that this matter of the relation between good and evil is clear-cut in either poet. Milton no more thought that the capacity for evil was limited to the bad angels than Vergil thought that the gods, if they existed, were simply wicked. Milton's understanding of the paradoxical relation of good and evil was expressed at *Paradise Lost* 4.222, "Knowledge of Good bought dear by knowing ill." The commentator's standard gloss on this line refers to a famous passage in *Areopagitica:*

> Good and evill we know in the field of this World grow up together almost inseparably; and the knowledge of good is so involv'd and interwoven with the knowledge of evill, and in so many cunning resemblances hardly to be discern'd, that those confused seeds which were impos'd on Psyche as an incessant labour to cull out, and sort, asunder, were not more intermixt. It was from out the rinde of one apple tasted, that the knowledge of good and evill as two twins cleaving together leapt forth into the World. And perhaps this is that doom which Adam fell into of knowing good and evill, that is to say of knowing good by evill.   (Wolfe, 2:514)

It is not easy to illustrate Vergil's views on the matter. There is probably in Jupiter's recognition of Juno as his "twin" something of the same paradox that Milton's image of good and

evil as twins demonstrates. Suffice it to say that even though
Vergil recognizes the presence of evil in the world and as-
cribes to it a divine origin, he also recognizes an imperative for
man to pursue order through political activity and to cultivate
piety toward the gods. This paradox is stated most strongly at
Aeneid 12.838–40, only a few lines after Jupiter has admitted
the "fluctus irarum" within Juno. He relents, grants her wish
that the Latins keep their name, customs, and language. Then
he concludes:

> hinc genus Ausonio mixtum quod sanguine surget,
> supra homines, supra ire deos pietate uidebis,
> nec gens ulla tuos aeque celebrabit honores.
>
> > (12.838–40)

> (From here a race mixed with Italian blood will rise,
>   which you will see surpass men and even the gods
>   in piety, and no nation will celebrate your honors as
>   they will.)

This new race, compounded from the native Latin stock and
the foreign Trojan blood, will *surpass even the gods* in piety, and
it will do this at least partly by worshiping Juno, the cause of
all their sorrows, more than she has ever been worshiped!

The question at 6.788 is a stronger allusion than the
question at 9.730: "Spirits" better translates "animis" than
"breasts." "Distempers," "perverseness," and "envy" are not a
close translation of "ira," though "ire" is among the "distempers" that beset Satan in the beginning of book 4. It would
seem that Milton is here simply embellishing or dilating upon
his original. But I suspect, rather, that he is reserving for his
own use the word that best translates Vergil's. In the proem

to book 9 of *Paradise Lost,* Milton claims that the narrative to
which he now turns is an

> argument
> Not less but more heroic than the wrath
> Of stern Achilles on his foe pursued
> Thrice fugitive around Troy wall; or rage
> Of Turnus for Lavinia disespoused,
> Or Neptun's ire or Juno's, that so long
> Perplexed the Greek and Cytherea's son.
>
> (9.13–19)

"Wrath" and "rage" are variants, rough synonyms, but notice
that "ire" proper is given to Neptune and Juno: Milton acknowledges the anger of Vergil's protagonist, Juno. But the
pagan gods are not the only ones who can get angry. In
the lines just before this quotation, Milton says he must now
speak of

> foul distrust, and breach
> Disloyal on the part of man, revolt
> And disobedience: on the part of heaven
> Now alienated, distance and distaste,
> *Anger* and just rebuke, and judgment given . . .
>
> (9.6–10, my emphasis)

Wrath, rage, ire, anger: call it what you will, it is still frighten-
ing to contemplate, in God or gods as in mortals.[55]

4

Quantum mutatus:
Language

> Nor does any thing, I conceive, require greater Skill or
> Delicacy, than to improve a Language by introducing
> foreign Treasures into it; the Words, so introduced,
> ought to be such, as, in a manner, naturalize them-
> selves; . . . otherwise, the Attempt will end in nothing
> but an uncouth unnatural Jargon, like the Phrase and
> Stile of *Milton,* which is a second Babel, or Confusion
> of all Languages.
> —Leonard Welsted, *Epistles, Odes, &c.*

Allusion and Translation

At the end of chapter 1, I suggested that the critical allusion
is a species of wit; I noted that, in fact, *allusion* is etymologi-
cally a kind of playing. This play no doubt has deep prehis-
toric roots, but historically it can be traced back almost to the
beginning of classical literature, and it seems to have a special association with the epic. The *Batrachomyomachia* or "Battle
of Frogs and Mice"—the title itself, of course, is parodic—is
an early lampoon of Homeric battle narratives. The stragegy
of its humor is quite simple and depends largely on what
I earlier called "reminiscence" (chapter 1). The language of
epic is transferred, that is, translated, to the world of the frog
pond; humor arises from the deliberate violation of linguis-

tic decorum.[1] Much later, the father of Roman satire, Lucilius (second century B.C.), by establishing the dactylic hexameter as the meter of satire, fixed a link between epic and satire that is hard to examine in the miserable fragments of Lucilius that remain, but is clearly discernible in Lucilius' epigones, Horace and Juvenal. A shocking example occurs in what is probably Horace's earliest, and certainly his nastiest, satire, 1.2:

> quidam notus homo cum exiret fornice, "macte
> uirtute esto" inquit sententia dia Catonis:
> "nam simul ac uenas inflauit taetra libido,
> huc iuuenes aequum est descendere, non alienas
> permolere uxores." "nolim laudarier" inquit
> "sic me" mirator cunni Cupiennius albi.
> Audire est operae pretium, procedere recte
> qui moechos non uoltis.
>
> (*Satires* 1.2.31–36)

My translation attempts to suggest the medley of tones:

> A certain young man of reputation was once seen exiting a brothel. "Blessed be thou!" was the divine Cato's greeting. "When filthy lust inflects the blood of young men, it is right that they should come down here, and not go banging other men's wives." But Cupiennius says, "Let me not be lauded thus!" His taste runs to higher-class cunt. *Oyez!* all ye who would fain have fornicators fail.

The Latin exhibits both stylistic reminiscence and genuine allusion. "Sententia dia Catonis" is formal and epic; a fragment of Lucilius has "Valeri sententia dia" (frag. 1240, Warmington). "Laudarier" is an archaic passive infinitive, used for epic effect. And Horace's scholiast informs us that the last line and a half parodies ("abutitur") a line from Ennius' historical epic, the *Annales:*

Audire est operae pretium procedere recte
qui rem Romanam Latiumque augescere uultis.
                        (frag. 471–72, Warmington)

(It is worth your while to lend an ear, all ye who wish the
    Roman state to move steadily forward and Latium to
    increase.)

This following directly on the obscenity "cunnus"! The clash
of sensibilities is deliberate. In other satires, Horace alludes
in similar fashion again and again to epic, and in *Satires* 2.5
he produces a full-scale parody by extracting the Homeric
Ulysses from his epic milieu and dropping him into an alien
world, the world of Latin. Not only do we hear of Penates and
Lares, augurs, *testamenta, heredes* and *coheredes* named Quintus
and Publius, slaves named Dama or Davus (from the Roman
stage), and so on; what is worse, Ulysses—still decked out in
the epic garb of the dactylic hexameter—is reduced to speaking in a colloquial style that is not only prosy, but almost vulgar. (Petronius' Croton episode deals with the same theme,
legacy hunting, but there is a world of difference between the
way Petronius treats the theme and the way it is handled by
Horace.) Poetry is made of words, not just ideas.

Some sort of translation in essential to this process whereby
old wine is put into new jars. The example from Horace's
Satire 1.2 involved *intra*lingual translation, from the old Latin
master Ennius. Intralingual translation was the only kind that
Apollonius Rhodius knew.[2] But in Rome and afterward, at
least in the practice of the greatest poets, this process in epic
usually involves *inter*lingual translation, from one language to
another. Indeed, the strategy is based on the exploitation of
the problem besetting all ordinary translation, namely, the incommensurability of the terms of one language with the terms

of another. For the ordinary translator this incommensurability is a matter of desperate and dire consequence: it means that the terms of the translator's language are always inadequate to the terms of the original. But for the creative poet this is an ironic advantage. The poet asserts that the terms of the new language are *more than adequate* to the terms of the earlier language. In fact, the later master is motivated to undertake epic precisely by the recognition that the terms of the earlier authoritative poem are no longer adequate to the poet's experience.

The Romans were the first to exploit this potential because they were the first Europeans to be bilingual, or at least the first Europeans for whom translation was a problem of abiding consequence. (The Greeks by and large regarded other languages—including Latin—as beneath them; people who did not speak Greek were *barbaroi,* "barbarians.") Now it is a commonplace of Roman literary history to observe that Latin literature begins with a translation, Livius Andronicus' version of the *Odyssey;* and translation continues to play a profoundly important part in later Latin literature. But after the second century B.C., translation's place in Roman culture was fairly different from its place in our own. Cicero's translations of the speeches of Greek orators or the Alexandrian Aratus' *Phainomena* were intended as vehicles for the adaptation in Latin of certain virtues or excellences of Greek writing. They were not primarily intended to make these works available to a large audience of readers who were ignorant of Greek, for such an audience did not exist. No doubt there were upper-class Romans whose Greek was less than fluent, but in general it seems safe to say that any contemporary of Cicero's who would have had an interest in Aratus could have read him in Greek. In fact, a Roman writer had to choose to write in his native language in a way that an ancient Greek did not. Cicero, after failing to persuade the Greek poet Archias to do the job for him, wrote in Greek (as well as in Latin) a memoir (*commentarii*) of his own consulship in 63. These works do not survive; but Cicero's correspondence is sprinkled liberally with bits of Greek, especially the letters to his best friend, Titus Pomponius, called "Atticus" because of his fondness for Athens.[3]

It is not the fact that much of early Latin literature involves direct or ordinary translation from Greek, then, that accounts for the Romans' primacy in the development of the sort of allusive wit involving translation that I am discussing. It is, rather, that once Latin literature reached maturity (by the second half of the first century B.C.), its writers were able to play against Greek while writing Latin: that is, they could expect their educated readers not just to call to mind the Greek targets of specific allusions, but to be aware of aspects of Greek diction, grammar, and style that they might imitate in Latin. What is genuinely interesting about these translations, in other words, will only be apparent to someone who knows the originals in their own language.

There seem to be two basic ways for writers to acknowledge the other language in whose shadow they are writing: by the adoption of words from that language, and by the imitation of certain features of its grammar or syntax. Latin authors do both of these things. The abandonment of native meters fairly early on and their replacement with the quantitative prosody of Greek was a matter of wholesale imitation that had lasting consequences. At the same time, certain early writers felt free to import Greek words as needed. Lucretius complains that the vocabulary of Latin is poor, and Cicero joins him in his philosophical writing in coining terms on the model of Greek ones or simply borrowing the words from Greek. As

Latin literature came to maturity, it began to eschew the use
of Greek words. Horace in *Satires* 1.10 criticizes Lucilius for
having mixed together Greek and Latin terms and suggests
that even if one might do this occasionally in verse, it certainly
would not be acceptable in court (20–35).[4] Cicero's speeches
do fairly scrupulously avoid the use of Greek that he allows
himself in his letters. Julius Caesar was praised by Cicero in
the *Brutus* for his pure *Latinitas,* and this is often acknowledged by the ancient authorities as one of the chief virtues
of style.[5] Even so, imitation of features of the Greek language
continued. Horace's introduction of Greek lyric meters into
Latin was one of his proudest achievements; and many features of the syntax and grammar of Vergil's *Aeneid* are based
on Greek.

The "Latinity" of Milton's style and especially his diction—
the simultaneous reminiscence of Latin style and acknowledgment of its alienness—is an important dimension of Milton's
intertextual or interlingual strategy. Now a lot of nonsense
has been written about the Latinity of Milton's diction—his
"Latinisms." Thomas N. Corns minimizes the Latinate effect
of Miltonic coinages such as "displode" and "congratulant,"
observing that the constituent parts of these words—the pre-
fixes, suffixes, and word roots—existed in English already;
Milton simply combined old elements in a new way to create
a word whose novelty is more technical than real.[6] But historical novelty is not the important point: perception is. W. B.
Hunter has noted that the eighteenth century felt strongly that
Milton's diction was frequently novel, even uncouth, while the
twentieth century has felt just as strongly that Milton's coinages are few.[7] But, observes Hunter, our sense that Milton's
diction is largely familiar English is a consequence of the fact
that Milton's contributions to the language have since the eigh-

teenth century been assimilated into common or at least accepted literary usage.[8] I would add that at the same time, the general reader's familiarity with Latin has steadily waned. This makes a difference in our ability to appreciate Milton's classical references and to distinguish between the greater and the lesser forms. Corns remarks that "horrent" in the phrase "horrent arms" (*Paradise Lost* 2.513) "perhaps proposes a Virgilian intertext," namely, "horrentibus hastis" (*Aeneid* 10.178). I doubt this. That Milton's usage is deliberately Latinate seems certain, and I think we can even find a better precedent for it than Vergil.[9] But in any case, this is not a true reference, that is, Milton is engaged here in appropriation or perhaps imitation rather than allusion. Rather than associating this Miltonic phrase with any particular target in Latin epic, we are supposed to respond to the Latinate effect of "horrent"—in so far as we are able.[10]

I suspect we should pay more attention to the eighteenth-century authorities, such as Welsted, who judged that Milton's diction is "a second Babel, or Confusion of all Languages" (quoted above as epigraph),[11] or Dr. Johnson, whose view that Milton "writ no language" is infamous. Welsted and Johnson are wrong to criticize Milton for this, but they do correctly perceive what is happening. An eighteenth-century reader educated in the classics would have treated Milton's text as a kind of linguistic palimpsest: the reader would be constantly aware of a dimension of classical syntax and diction just beneath the English itself. What is odd, however, is that the top level is referring to the level that it overlays. Spenser, from whom Milton learned so much, antiqued his English, but it remained English. Milton's strategy is more profound. He writes English that is constantly pointing beyond itself to something else, or perhaps I should say that it is *playing against* something that does not appear to be there, like Marcel Marceau leaning on a wall that is invisible, but solidly suggested by his pantomime.

Dobson's Paradisus Amissus

Since this aspect of Milton's allusiveness is general rather than local, no description that I could give of its effect will be compelling. Instead, in what follows I will consider the problem from a different perspective, one that may seem backward or upside-down, by asking, What if *Paradise Lost* had been written in Latin? The hypothesis is not fantastic. It is a queer fact of literary history—if *fact* is the right word—that *Paradise Lost*, one of the most indigenous treasures of the English language, might very well have been written in Latin. Milton's earliest flirtation with epic, the poem on the Gunpowder Plot, *In Quintum Novembris,* is in polished Latin hexameters. Indeed, Latin is the language of the majority of Milton's poetry (excepting *Comus*) written before 1640 or so, and at least one of these early productions, the *Epitaphium Damonis,* deserves to be considered alongside anything he wrote before *Paradise Lost.* Furthermore, the majority of his prose from any period is in what is arguably the most accomplished Latin of the seventeenth century.[12] In other words, a knowledge of Milton's writings that ignores his Latin is dangerously partial. That the final choice of English for his major poems was not inevitable, but truly deliberate, appears from his repeated references to the matter over a long period of time, for example, in "At a Vacation Exercise" (1628), lines 29–32; in *Epitaphium Damonis* (1639), lines 168–78; in the preface to book 2 of *The Reason of Church Government* (1642); and elsewhere.

What would *Paradise Lost* have been like as a Neo-Latin poem? Very fortunately, we need not construct a Latin *Paradise Lost* for ourselves to study; the work has been done for us,

several times over, in fact. In the century following the publication of *Paradise Lost* in 1667, there appeared in print well
over a dozen attempts to translate all or part of the poem in
Latin hexameters; there were also a couple of Greek attempts.
To me, the best of these Latin translations is that of a certain William Dobson, a minor poet who undertook the project
on commission.[13] As must frequently have been the case in
the eighteenth century, Dobson wrote better Latin verse than
English, and his *Paradisus Amissus,* published in Oxford and
London in the mid-eighteenth century, is literarily rather successful.[14] It will be possible for us to nitpick Dobson profitably
without arrogance or pretense of superior skills. Would that
any of us could write Latin so fluent, if so flawed!

This is how Dobson begins:

> Primam Hominis Noxam, vetitâque ex Arbore fœtus
> Avulsos, morsu quæ degustata nefando
> Humanæ genti mortem & genus omne malorum
> Intulit, & miseros *Edeni* sedibus egit,
> Donec Progenies Humano ab semine Major
> Restituat lapsos, lætisque reponat in arvis,
> Diva canas.

At the real risk of misleading the Latinless reader more than
helping, I shall attempt to translate Dobson's translations, as
"literally" as possible:

> Sing, Goddess, the original crime of mankind, the fruits
> picked from the forbidden tree which, once tasted with a
> blasphemous bite, brought death upon the human race and
> every kind of woe and drove them wretched from the seat of
> Eden, until a greater offspring from mankind's seed should
> restore them whence they slipped and replace them in the
> happy fields.

I know my English sounds wordy, but Dobson's Latin, though running one line longer than Milton's English, is pretty economical.[15] "Loss of Eden" seems to have stumped him; "amissio" will not go into dactylic hexameter. But "damnum Edeni" would have done well, and greater economy and literalness could have been had, viz.:

> intulit et damnum Edeni, dum restituat nos
> unus homo maior ponatque in sede beata.

Dobson's "genus omne malorum" is odd for "all our woe." Later, when Milton repeats this motivic phrase, Dobson uses the obviously right word. Sin is about to unlock Hell's gates:

> Thus saying, from her side the fatal key,
> Sad instrument of all our woe, she took.
>   (2.871–72)

Dobson writes:

> Dixerat: & Clavem demissam à pectore, Clavem
> Horrendam, unde omnes nostri fluxêre dolores,
> Corripit.
>   (vol. 1, p. 91)

> (She finished speaking, and took the key hanging on her
> chest, the frightful key, whence all our woes ["dolores"]
> have flowed.)

"Dolorum" would have been better for "woe" in the first place, that is, back in the proem. But looking again at the earlier line, "Humanae genti mortem & genus omne malorum," one can understand Dobson's choice: his "mortem . . . malorum" echoes the alliteration of "world . . . woe." So this fault may actually be a kind of virtue. He succeeds in giving a similar rhetorical effect even when his translation is not lexically exact.

Here is Dobson handling another famous passage:

> Not that fair field
> Of Enna, where Proserpine gathering flowers
> Her self a fairer flower by gloomy Dis
> Was gathered.
>
>   (4.268–71)

>   Non his Paradisi
> Deliciis prædulce solum certaverit Ennæ,
> Filia quà *Cereris* periit, dum gramine molli
> Formosos legeret flores formosior ipsa.
>
>   (vol. 1, pp. 157–58)

(With these delights of Paradise the sweet soil of Enna
did not compete, Enna, where the daughter of Ceres
perished as she picked beautiful flowers in the soft
grass, herself more beautiful still.)

Proserpina's name is omitted, and various aspects of Milton's English wordplay are lost, but not without compensation. Instead of "flowers . . . flower" we get "formosos . . . formosior"; there is an increase in alliteration here, as in the English; "*Cereris*" resonates with "solum" and especially "gramine." Dobson enjambs his lines nearly as often as Milton, and more than either Vergil or Ovid. He strives everywhere to follow the sinuous form of Milton's periods; he is a pretty skillful Latin prosodist; and he shows care as an interpreter of Milton's difficult English. Hard passages in the original, which William Hog, for example, the author of the first complete Latin translation (1690) and a Neo-Latin poet in his own right, generally steps around (not always gracefully), are usually met straight on by Dobson and rendered with intelligence and precision.

No doubt certain local effects would have defied any attempt at translation. For Milton's climactic apostrophe to the prelapsarian Adam and Eve in book 4,

> Sleep on
> Blest pair; and O yet happiest if ye seek
> No happier state, and know to know no more,
>   (4.773–75)

Dobson gives,

> Molles etiamnum ô ducite somnos,
> Par felix, nimium ô felix, si gaudia rerum
> Vestrarum nôstis penitùs, nec quæritis ultrà.
>   (vol. 1, p. 186)

> (O, stay on in your sweet sleep, equally happy, only too happy, if you know the joys of your circumstances inwardly, and do not search further.)

Milton's paronomasia depends on the simplicity, the brevity of his words; Latin could not do it. Moreover, Dobson's version here and elsewhere suffers from a general flatness that all honest translations betray. I say this only to concede that Dobson's translation is an imperfect model of what Milton himself would have written in Latin. Nevertheless, it is good enough to suggest some of the ways that a Neo-Latin *Paradise Lost* would be essentially different from the poem we have.

"Quantum mutatus ab illo"

Let us return now to the differences between Milton's poem and our hypothetical *Paradisus Amissus*. All of the differences between the two are linguistic in some way.

I pass over a couple of differences that are fairly obvious, though not without interest. The prosody, for example: the dactylic hexameter is a tremendously more restrictive verse form than the one Milton chose for his English poem.[16] Milton's English prosody was daringly innovative, but a Neo-Latin *Paradise Lost* could not have been so, because the conventions of the hexameter were too restrictive and too fixed. The freedom that Milton flaunts, not without irony, in his first line, "Of man's first disobedience, and the fruit," was thematically significant for him, as one can infer from the political overtones in the note on "The Verse," where he speaks of "ancient liberty recovered to heroic poem." True, he is referring to freedom from the "bondage" of rhyme and cites Homer and Vergil as exemplary; but I do not doubt that the syllabic and accentual liberty he arrogated to his verse is significant as well, even if it is not ancient.

Another aspect of the differences that I pass over is grammar—by which I mean the more mechanical differences between English and Latin. Here again Latin is more restrictive. For example, "Diva canas" in Dobson's proem for "Sing heavenly Muse," is fine, but the unavoidable specification of the gender is somewhat regrettable. In English, too, Muses are presumably female most of the time, but a "heavenly Muse" is a rare type, and there remains a degree of deliberate indefiniteness in the relationship of the "heavenly Muse" to the "Spirit," who is presumably masculine.

Leaving these differences, then, I turn to a couple that seem more fundamentally important. First, there is Milton's calculated use of a Latinate word in a context deliberately inappropriate to the moral connotations that the word has acquired in English.[17] This is another sort of allusion in the general sense that I have described. Ironically these Latinisms cannot be translated into Latin. Here, in an excerpt from Satan's first address in Hell to the fallen angels, "virtue" is obviously not a godly power:

> have ye chosen this place
> After the toil of battle to repose
> Your wearied virtue. . . ?
>
> (1.318–20)

Dobson renders this passage, naturally enough:

> Sed fortè libet decumbere fluctu,
> Scilicet hìc Virtus bellis ut lassa quiescat . . .
>
> (vol. 1, p. 18)

> (But perchance you would like to recline from the
> melée, so that here your war-wearied *virtue* might rest.)

That *virtus* did acquire a possible moral sense before the end of
the classical period is beside the point. It did not require that
sense, and there is nothing necessarily ironic about "Virtus" as
Dobson uses it here. Actually this effect can be achieved even
with non-Latinate words. Notice the strangely repressed force
of "fell," "nether," and perhaps even "flood" and "darksome"
in this description of the prelapsarian Garden:

> Upon the rapid current, which through veins
> Of porous earth with kindly thirst up drawn,
> Rose a fresh fountain, and with many a rill
> Watered the garden; thence united fell
> Down the steep glade, and met the nether flood,
> Which from his darksome passage now appears.
>
> (4.227–32)

There is not a hint of ominous overtone in Dobson's Latin:

> Unde recens venis terræ sitientibus haustus
> Fons hortis salit irriguis, multoque meatu
> Hinc atque hinc placidarum erumpit rivus aquarum.

Tum per præcipitem clivum simul agmine facto
Subjectum in Fluvium rapido sese impete volvunt,
Tramite qui tandem tenebroso emergit ad auras . . .

(vol. 1, p. 155)

(whence a fresh fountain drawn up from the thirsty
veins of the Earth leaps through the well-watered gar-
dens, and from many a passageway the river of peaceful
waters breaks. Then down the steep bank suddenly in
line the waters with swift force roll themselves into the
flood below, which finally emerges from its shadowy
course to the air . . .)

A few lines later Milton describes the course of the brooks,
"with mazy error," which becomes simply "errarent" in Dobson's Latin.

The Latinisms suggest quite clearly that much of the force
and interest of Milton's poetry comes precisely from the re-
sistance offered by the native character of English to Milton's
constant impulse to reform it along classical lines. In book 4
again, notice the passage in which Gabriel is giving orders to
two of the angels guarding Eden:

Ithuriel and Zephon, with winged speed
Search through this garden, leave unsearched no nook,
But chiefly where those two fair creatures lodge,
Now laid perhaps asleep secure of harm.
This evening from the sun's decline arrived
Who tells of some infernal spirit seen
Hitherward bent (who could have thought?) escaped
The bars of hell, on errand bad no doubt:
Such where ye find, seize fast, and hither bring.

(4.788–96)

This tension is felt neither in Shakespeare, where no attempt at grammatical redesign is made, nor in Pope, where the attempt has already succeeded utterly and the language no longer resists. It is not surprising that the English Romantics who sought to recover "natural" English diction should have been so fascinated with Milton, who had striven in precisely the other direction. He and they were merely looking at different ends of the same problem.

Another aspect of Milton's poetry for which my Neo-Latin hypothesis has serious consequences is its engagement of other texts, that is, its allusiveness. While Milton's Greek appears to have been as good as that of any of his contemporaries and his allusions to Greek—as shown in earlier chapters—can be deeply penetrating, the majority of his classical allusions are to Latin authors. Furthermore (and I hope my classical colleagues will forgive me for this heresy), from the perspective of English poetry, Greek and Latin are, while hardly indistinguishable, at least very similar. (It is the failure to acknowledge this *relative* similarity, I am sure, that has confused debates about whether the classical elements of Milton's style owe more to Greek or to Latin.) Alluding in Latin to Vergil and Horace, or even Hesiod and Homer, is not the same thing at all as alluding to them in a modern and quite radically different language such as English.

For an example one need look no further than the first crucial Vergilian allusion in the poem, early in book 1. Beelzebub recognizes the fallen Satan and addresses him:

> If thou beest he; but O how fallen! how changed
> From him, who in the happy realms of light
> Clothed with transcendent brightness didst outshine
> Myriads though bright.
>
> (1.84–87)

Milton is alluding to the splendid dream-narrative in *Aeneid* 2, where Hector's ghostly image appears to Aeneas:

> ei mihi, qualis erat, quantum mutatus ab illo
> Hectore qui redit exuuias indutus Achilli.
>
> (2.274–75)

> (Oh my! What a shape he was in! How changed from
>   that Hector who had once returned dressed in the spoils
>   of Achilles.)

"Qualis erat," whose indefiniteness might more precisely be suggested by the translation "what sort of man he was," becomes strongly thematic for Milton, "how fallen," making Milton's other phrase, the fairly exact "how changed"—which is the key to the recognition of the allusion—more meaningful in English than it had been in Vergil's Latin. It points not simply to Satan's tragically altered appearance, but to an absolute change in his moral condition, reflecting a kind of spiritual death. Translation into English renders the basic sense of change responsive to a new moral context. But this is almost impossible to see when the allusion is framed in Vergil's own language as used by Dobson:

> Si sis ille Idem! verùm ô quàm eversus, ab Illo
> Quantùm ô mutatus, lætis qui lucis in oris
> Tot rutilorum unus superabas millia longè
> Cœlicolùm, eximio radiorum indutus amictu!
>
> (vol. 1, p. 6)

> (If only you might be the great man himself! But O, how
>   overturned, how greatly changed from him who in the
>   happy regions of light surpassed by far so many thou-
>   sands of the bright offspring of heaven, clothed yourself
>   in the priceless garb of radiance.)

One can see certain elements of Vergil's diction here. But "eversus" has none of the resonance of "fallen," and consequently Dobson fails to invest "mutatus" with the moral depth that Milton's "how changed" had acquired. Vergil's words are brought to mind, but neither the local pathos nor the larger context of the Vergilian passage is evoked and reconsidered, as it had been in Milton's English allusion. I have found this failure to be common to all the passages in which Dobson translates what had been for Milton in English a critical allusion. I also suspect it is typical of the Vergilian imitations in such master Neo-Latin poets as Sannazaro, Mantuan, or the young Milton himself.

Consider another example, an allusion at once simpler and much more pregnant with meaning than the last. As was suggested in chapter 2, the opening of Milton's book 7 involves a crucially important allusion to Horace's great Roman ode beginning "Descende caelo" (*Carmina* 3.4). Of course, "Descende caelo," which begins an Alcaic stanza, will not go straight into a dactylic hexameter, but "Descende, Vrania, e caelo" is a fairly obvious transposition that has nothing serious against it. (It uses a little more elision than post-Vergilian writers usually liked, but that would not have troubled Dobson.) So when I first looked at Dobson's book, I wondered why he chose instead to write "Labere Diva polo" (vol. 2, p. 1). For one thing, elsewhere he uses the verb *labor* ("glide" or "slide") and its cognates, such as *lapsus,* in the morally unfavorable sense, as one might say in English, "So-and-so is a lapsed Catholic." And "polo" for "heaven" seems wrong.

But these are quibbles compared to the way he has destroyed the allusion. It is unlikely that he simply did not see it. It had been noted in Bishop Newton's first variorum commentary, published in 1749, four years before Dobson's volume

containing book 7. It is almost unthinkable that he should have
failed to consult Newton, and in any case, the allusion should
have been self-evident. Or again, perhaps he recognized it but
did not reckon it to be very significant.

There is a third possibility, however, and I consider it likelier than either of the foregoing. It is that in these examples,
as elsewhere throughout Dobson's poem, Milton's interpretative allusions, which depend so much on creative translation
into English, have been reduced to instances of mere *imitatio*,
in accord with a principle expressed by Vida in *De Arte Poetica:*

> et raptus memor occule versis
> verborum indiciis, atque ordine falle legentes
> mutato; nova sit facies, nova prorsus imago.
> Munere (nec longum tempus) vix ipse peracto
> dicta recognosces veteris mutata poetae.
>   (3.218–22)[18]

(Don't forget to cover up your thefts by changing the
traces of the words, and by altering their order deceive
your readers. By all means let your verse have a novel
appearance, a novel image. If you have performed this
task (and it should not take long), you yourself will have
difficulty recognizing the transformed phrases of the
ancient poet.)

Vida, of course, illustrates his point with a subtle reworking here of the famous line of Dido to her sister when she
realizes that she is falling in love with Aeneas, "agnosco uete-
ris uestigia flammae" (*Aeneid* 4.23: "I recognize the traces of
the ancient flame"), but one should note that Vida's imitation
neither attempts nor achieves the depth of contextual correspondence typical of Milton's critical allusions. Vida's "vix,"

which means "hardly" both in the sense of "scarcely" and
of "with difficulty," is carefully chosen, as is the possessive
genitive "poetae." His advice is not to make the phrases your
own. The "dicta" remain the property of the old poet, but are
subtly disguised—not so much as to be unrecognizable, for
that would defeat the entire point, but so that recognition is
difficult ("vix").

The aim of Milton's critical allusions has relatively little to
do with *imitatio* as Vida understood and practiced it so bril-
liantly. From the beginning of chapter 1, I have been arguing
that Milton's principal concern is always hermeneutic rather
than imitative. To be sure, every page of his poetry displays
his imitative genius as well, which was at least equal to Vida's.
But I believe that the critical allusions, which as I said above
are relatively rare, are designed to call to mind not just a line
or two from a model text, but the entire context, and sometimes, by implication, the entire work. The pre-text is alluded
to because it is preeminently authoritative as one of the privi-
leged sources of the wisdom of our culture. But a critical allusion must do more than refer to the authoritative pre-text. It
must at the same time intimate the profound chasm between
Milton's experience (modern, Christian, English) and the experience embodied in the pre-text (ancient, pagan, Roman
or Greek).

I submit that this twofold task—that is, first reference, then
critique—cannot be adequately performed without translation of some sort. Neo-Latin imitation employs not just any
Latin, but precisely Vergil's or Ovid's or Horace's Latin, insofar
as possible. Contrast the intralingual allusions of a poet such as
T. S. Eliot, whose concerns are closer to Milton's. Making critical allusion to earlier English poetry, Eliot will simply quote his
source verbatim, as he did, to take an example from *The Waste*

Land, in Webster's "O keep the dog far hence, that's friend to men"—that is, without any attempt to disguise the source by reconstituting its phrases. Or if he does rework the original, he does not imitate the English of the period of the target text, as, to cite *The Waste Land* again, this reworking of Marvell:

> But at my back from time to time I hear
> The sound of horns and motors, which shall bring
> Sweeney to Mrs. Porter in the spring.

Eliot's method, in other words, is parodic and closely resembles the method of Horace is his *Satires,* illustrated above. Milton, on the other hand, is able in some ways to keep quite close to the sense and grammatical construction of his target line or phrase and yet effect an interpretative transmutation simply by virtue of the recasting of the original in an alien language, expressing a radically alien sensibility.

All of this leads to the fundamental mystery of linguistic difference. I regard it as axiomatic that certain things cannot be said in certain languages. I would further maintain that the essential qualities of *Paradise Lost* could not be reproduced in Latin, not even if Milton himself had been the author. I rather doubt that they could be reproduced in any other European language. The vocabulary of the Romance languages is too deeply bound to Latin, while the German vocabulary (not to mention the vocabularies of the northern European countries) is too remote from it. Milton's language is Latinate in several ways, it is true. He employs long, complicated rhetorical periods and displays a predilection for difficult, strange, usually classically derived words. But one should not lose sight of the fundamentally simple language that underlies those baroque embellishments and that keeps Milton's poetry from being unbearably precious. Many of his thematic words are

unregenerately Anglo-Saxon: *stand, fall, woe.* Even those derived ultimately from Latin had long since been naturalized
in English and lack the Latin ring. *fruit, obey.*

These thematic words presented a special problem to Dobson. All are resonant with meanings in English that the obvious translations in Latin do not naturally have. Now I must
admit that it is by no means certain how one should understand the meanings of many words used by Neo-Latin authors.
That is, it does seem possible that a Neo-Latin author may
use an ordinary Latin word with an awareness of the modern
vernacular word behind it, and thus the effect intended and
achieved in, say, the seventeenth century would be slightly different from the effect that the very same words would have
had in Cicero's time. Dobson thus uses *cado* ("fall") frequently,
presumably with a Biblical resonance that Vergil never heard.

On the other hand, some English words that are important to Milton simply have no Latin equivalents. The most
important of these, surely, is *obedience. Oboedio* and *oboedien-
tia* are found in classical prose, in Cicero and Livy for example, but are not especially common; and in most inflectional
forms neither verb nor noun will fit into the hexameter, so
they are not found at all in the poets. *Pareo* does not really
mean the same thing as *oboedio,* and in any case it lacks a cognate noun. Translating the opening words of the poem, "Of
Man's First Disobedience," Dobson gives "Primam Hominis
Noxam."[19] Later, in book 5, in a dense passage where the word
obedience recurs several times in close proximity, Dobson is at
a loss. Adam is seeking clarification from Raphael:

> But say,
> What meant that caution joined, *If ye be found
> Obedient?* Can we want obedience then
> To him, or possibly his love desert

Who formed us from the dust, and placed us here
Full to the utmost measure of what bliss
Human desires can seek or apprehend?
    To whom the angel. Son of heaven and earth,
Attend: that thou art happy, owe to God;
That thou continuest such, owe to thyself,
That is, to thy obedience; therein stand.

                        (5.512–22)

In Dobson's Latin, this passage becomes:

Quò verò hi spectant Monitus, Mandata Supremi
Si colitis memores?—Nosne adversabimur Illi?
Illius unquamne exciderit de pectore nostro
Dulcis Amor, luteo qui primum è pulvere finxit,
Qui dedit has sedes, dotesque indulsit amœnas,
Quantum extrema Hominum poscat sitiatque libido?
    Cui placidus contra sic Nuntius: ô sata cœlo
Progenies terrisque, hæc jam mea percipe dicta.
Dona dedit tibi tanta DEUS; Tu propria faxis:
Jussa pius serves; hoc stas fundamine solo.

                        (vol. 1, p. 230)

(But what does this warning mean, *if you cherish the will
of the Almighty in your memory?* Shall we set ourselves
against Him? Will our hearts ever let fall the sweet love
of Him who first fashioned us from the filthy dust, who
gave us this homeland, showered kindly gifts upon us,
to such measure as the most extreme craving of mankind might hunger and thirst for.
    To whom the peaceful messenger thus responds: O
offspring born of Heaven and Earth, take to heart what
now I say. GOD has given you these great gifts; you must

make them your own. Devotedly ["pius"] you must keep
his commands; on this foundation alone you stand.)

A few lines later, alluding to the disobedience of the rebel
angels (whose story he has not yet told), Raphael says,

> And some are fallen, to disobedience fallen,
> And so from heaven to deepest hell; O fall
> From what high state of bliss into what woe!
>   (5.541–43)

The syntax of "to disobedience" in the first line presents a
problem to the Latin translator: it is obviously not place-to-
which (which would take the accusative), but cause (taking the
ablative) seems not quite right either. Dobson evades the word
"disobedience" altogether:

> Pars nostrum haud pridem cecidere, è tramite vero
> Collapsi, à summo vel ad infima Tartara cœlo:
> Quam lætà ô quantos mutarunt arce dolores!
>   (vol. 1, p. 231)

> (Some of our number not long ago have fallen, slipped
>   from the true path, from the top of Heaven to the bot-
>   tom of Tartarus. How great are the woes for which they
>   have traded this blessed citadel!)

Such problems equally face the modern translator of an ancient language: how to render *pietas* in Vergil, *humanitas* in
Cicero, θέμις or ἀρετή in Homer? But they are, finally, only
the most evident instances of linguistic difference. I suspect
that such problems exist almost everywhere; and while they
may usually be much less consequential, ten thousand minor
misrepresentations cannot help but add up to a grand, comprehensive betrayal.

Sannazaro, Imitation, and Allusion

I have already suggested that Milton's allusive strategy depends upon translating the predecessor's—that is, preeminently, Vergil's—narrative and ethical situations into a new linguistic context that is inhospitable to them. Since the antipathy between the Biblical and the classical designs of *Paradise Lost* is perhaps the major generator of the poem's meaning, and since the context provided in Dobson's Latin is in many ways not inhospitable to Vergil, it is obvious that a Neo-Latin *Paradise Lost* would at a minimum relate very differently to its Scriptural pre-texts. They would, it seems likely, be put at a disadvantage. So much is at stake here that it seems appropriate not to rely too much on William Dobson's translation. Having digressed from Milton's English text this far, I want to leave it behind completely for a few pages and consider how problems very similar to Milton's were dealt with in Latin by a writer who was not a mere translator but a genuine poet, Jacopo Sannazaro.

The tension between the Christian and the classical or pagan dimensions in Sannazaro's *De Partu Virginis* (1526) has been noticed since the poem was written. W. Leonard Grant, after giving a résumé of the poem, says:

> Even from a brief summary it is obvious what it is that has made many a reader uncomfortable: Sannazaro's inveterate paganism. It is true that this poet writes the most limpid and technically proficient verse of any of the Italian Neo-Latinists; his gentle hexameters are almost invariably flawless. But the constant use of pagan elements is frequently incongruous in a biblical setting: Sannazaro's Hell contains Cerburus, Tisiphone, and the other horrors of ancient mythology; Vida's has the Devil himself.[20]

It is significant that Grant thinks that this objection can be raised on the basis of his summary, and equally significant that he thinks that Vida is innocent of the fault for which he is indicting Sannazaro. It is a mistake, however, to think that the problem is simply that Sannazaro admits a few mythological characters. As Charles Fantazzi observes, Sannazaro does not go so far as his predecessor Mantuan had in his *Parthenice,* referring to Christ as Apollo or the Virgin as the "Palestinian nymph." In fact, says Fantazzi, "The classical figures of [Sannazaro's] poem are not mere ornaments, but almost instruments of divine revelation."[21] And even if it were as simple a matter as Grant has it, we could in any event enjoy those numerous parts of the poem that do not explicitly mention pagan figures, and it would seem that critics should have found Vida's *Christiad* less blameworthy in this regard, since his poem provides no cameo roles for the figures of pagan myth. As it is, however, the critics tend to be just as unhappy—or even unhappier—with Vida.

The real problem is not mythological, but linguistic. I am not thinking merely of the classical or pagan elements in Sannazaro's vocabulary (Mary has "Penates" in her house; God is regularly referred to as "Iupiter" or "Tonans"; and so on). And I am not thinking of the style in a superficial sense, as is David Quint, who, after observing that Sannazaro committed himself to following his Biblical sources, remarks, "The task which is left to [Sannazaro] is essentially one of style, of decoration and embellishment."[22] What the *De Partu Virginis* actually *is* I shall get to shortly, but it is *not* an illuminated manuscript, putting the plain text of scripture front and center and simply framing it with classical "decorations" and "embellishments." When I say that the problem is with the language, I am thinking of the *medium* in its fullest sense, which includes, among other things, the pagan quintessence of the dactylic hexameter verse, the style that comes with it and the values that style implies, and the elevated Latin diction generally. I want to make it clear that, although I think it right to speak of a "problem," I believe nevertheless that the delicately pagan complexion of Sannazaro's verses is the quality that saves them from being merely good imitations and constitutes their peculiar excellence. The problem, then, is a critical or interpretative one, not a poetic one.

The tension can be found almost anywhere in the poem. Fantazzi observes, for example, of Gabriel's "Ave, Maria" that "The simple salutation of the angel seems to have resisted easy translation into classical verse."[23] He notes that in the pre-1526 earlier version of the first book, the angel says, "Salve, o nostris lux addita rebus" ("Hail, O Light granted to our affairs"); in the final edition, on the other hand, we find "Oculis salve lux debita nostris" (1.109: "Hail, Light owed to our eyes"). But "Ave, o Maria" would have fit into a hexameter, if Sannazaro had been that interested in "accuracy." I think the tension is most evident in the speeches of Mary. Consider, for example, this passage in which she apostrophizes Gabriel as he reascends to Heaven after the Annunciation:

> "Magne ales, celsi decus ætheris, invia rerum
>   qui penetras longeque et nubila linquis et euros
>   antevolans; læto seu te et felicia tractu
>   sidera quæque suos volvuntur signa per orbes
>   expectant redeuntem; alti seu certa reposcit
>   crystalli domus et vitrei plaga lucida regni;
>   seu propiora vocant supremo tecta Tonanti,
>   qua patet in summum regio flammantis Olympi
>   teque amor et liquidis flagrans alit ignibus aura:

i, precor, i, nostrum testis defende pudorem."
Nec plura his.

> ("Great bird, glory of the high ether, you who pene-
> trate the pathless places of nature, flying before the
> winds and leaving the clouds behind: whether the stars,
> lucky in their happy path, await your return along with
> those constellations that turn in their own orbits; or
> whether it is the fixed home of the upper crystalline
> sphere and the bright region of the glassy kingdom;
> or whether the dwellings closer to the high Thunderer
> himself, where the region of fiery Olympus opens into
> the height and love and the breeze ardent with liquid
> fire nourish you—go, I pray, go, be a witness in defense
> of my chastity." And she said no more than this.)

Is this good poetry or bad? Shall we describe it as elegant and artful, or is it derivative and long-winded? Judging the tone here is terribly difficult. We may suspect it of being bad because these lines certainly are inconsistent with the Biblical picture of a simple young maiden. And yet the inconsistency provides a peculiarly artistic kind of pleasure. I detect a kind of irony here; could it be that there is even humor? "And she said no more than this" ("nec plura his")—but, heavens, she had said quite a mouthful already! Of course, Sannazaro is not Ovid, and I hesitate to accuse him of irreverence. Perhaps amusement is my own, inappropriate reaction.

Let us look more closely at another passage, also from the second book. It is Sannazaro's reworking of the Magnificat (Luke 1.46–55):

> Illa sub hæc: "Miranda alti quis facta Tonantis,
> o mater, meritas cælo quæ tollere laudes   50

vox queat? Exultant dulci mea pectora motu
auctori tantorum operum, qui me ima tenentem
indignamque humilemque suis respexit ab astris;
munere quo genteis felix ecce una per omnes
iam dicar. Nec vana fides: ingentia quando   55
ipse mihi ingenti cumulavit munera dextra
omnipotens; sanctumque eius per sæcula nomen
et quæ per magnas clementia dedita terras
exundat, qua passim omneis sua iussa verentes
usque fovens, nullo neglectos deserit ævo.   60
Tum fortem exertans humerum dextramque coruscam
insanos longe fastus menteisque superbas
dispulit afflixitque super solioque potentes
deturbans dedit in præceps et ad ima repressit;
extollensque humiles aliena in sede locavit.   65
Pauperiemque famemque fugans, implevit egenos
divitiis; vacuos contra nudosque reliquit,
qui nullas opibus metas posuere parandis.
Postremo sobolem (neque enim dare maius habebat)
omnibus æqualemque sibi, de sanguine fidi   70
suscepit pueri (tantis quod honoribus unum
deerat adhuc), non ille animi morumque suorum
oblitus, quippe id meditans promiserat olim
sacrificis proavorum atavis stirpique nepotum."   75

(De Partu Virginis 2.49–75)

(Mary replied [to Elizabeth]: "Who, O mother, might
exalt to Heaven the amazing deeds of the supernal
Thunderer? What voice might sing the praises he deserves? My heart with a sweet movement leaps up to the
author of such works. Though I am lowly and unde-
serving, a dweller in these lower regions, he has looked

down upon me from his home in the stars, and because of this favor, lo! I shall now be called blessed by
all nations. [55:] Nor is their faith empty, since with his
great right hand the Almighty himself has showered
on me great gifts. Let forever be holy his name and the
gifts that his mercy has poured forth throughout the
earth. With his mercy he still protects those everywhere
who fear his commandments; he has at no time deserted
them and left them helpless. [61:] Yet he has extended
the strength of his arm and his hand's brilliance to cast
far out all forms of mad disdainfulness and arrogance
of mind. He has struck down the powerful and knocked
them from their thrones, casting them headlong to the
lower regions and confining them there. And he has
filled their seats with the lowly whom he exalted. [66:]
Banishing poverty and hunger, he has enriched the
needy; but he has left empty and unclothed those who
put no limits on the acquisition of riches. [69:] Finally,
having nothing greater to give, he has acknowledged
as his own his eternal offspring, who existed before
the ages and is his equal in all things: an offspring of
the blood of the faithful boy [David], since to his great
honors this alone remains to be added. For he did not
forget his own mind's purposes, when long ago looking
forward he had promised this event to the pious fore-
fathers of the boy's ancestors and to the line of their
descendants.")

There are, of course, many changes from the Vulgate. For
one thing, the Neo-Latin version is a good bit longer and
more involved. In 69–72, Sannazaro expands four words from
the Vulgate, "suscepit Israhel puerum suum," into twenty-one

words extending for three and a half lines.[24] There are additions, some of them classicizing. Mary calls God "Thunderer" and describes him further as an agent or "auctor" of "facta" and "opera." The Lucan phrase, however, is simply: "Magnificat anima mea Dominum et exsultavit spiritus meus in Deo salutari meo." There are also curious omissions, such as the reference to God as savior in the Vulgate, which is not in any way paralleled in Sannazaro. And there is one especially interesting transformation of verse 53, "et divites dimisit inanes," with its vigorous, emphatic alliteration supporting a straightforward rejection of wealth, into "vacuos contra nudosque reliquit, / qui nullas opibus metas posuere parandis" (67–68: "but he has left empty and unclothed those who put no limits on the acquisition of riches"). In other words, it's okay to go after riches as long as you know when to say when.

There are significant differences in what might be called the personal dimension. Mary's motivation is less clear in Sannazaro's version. Luke goes on to explain *why* Mary is glorifying the Lord in two clauses introduced by "quia," with the emphatic "ecce enim" line (verse 48b) in between. Sannazaro considerably weakens this cause-and-effect relation between the opening sentence and what follows. He wants to give Mary her own motivation, I suspect; she is not just reacting, she is acting. Furthermore, the elaboration of the style in Sannazaro tends to destroy the direct personal relationship between God and Mary (or God and his people) that is the essence of the evangelist's text. Sannazaro's God looks down upon Mary from the stars ("suis respexit ab astris," 53); Luke simply has him noticing Mary's humility (verse 48). In Sannazaro, the extension of God's mercy in personal time, from generation to generation ("a progenie in progenies"), becomes an extension in impersonal space ("per magnas . . . terras"), and the mercy is bestowed on those who fear or revere his commands ("omneis sua iussa verentes"), while in the Gospel it is given to those who fear God himself ("timentibus eum").[25] The changes display an almost Miltonic touch.

But to observe these details is not to observe the most truly significant differences between the two versions of the passage, which are more radical. It is the language itself that counts for Sannazaro, the classical Latin, the dactylic hexameter, and the style that they entail. And it is at this level that the inconcinnity between style and content is loudest.

Sannazaro's Mary calls herself "indignamque humilemque" (line 53); the words call to mind Augustine's complaint about the style of the Bible:

> visa est mihi indigna, quam Tullianae dignitati conpararem. tumor enim meus refugiebat modum eius, et acies mea non penetrabat interiora eius.   (*Confessions* 3.5)

> (It seemed to me unworthy of comparison with the dignity of Cicero. My inflated sense of my own greatness recoiled from its restraint, and my glance did not penetrate to its interior.)

One wonders, reading Sannazaro, in what respect Mary is unworthy. The language is the only thing to which we can refer for judgment, but it in no way points beyond itself to the unreachable grandeur of God or the ineffable mysteries of his purposes. Sannazaro does not confess, as Dante had, that words fail him. On the other hand, nothing in the language suggests that Mary herself is inadequate. At a minimum, she seems to have had a very good education and to be accustomed to thinking about matters both complex and subtle. On the contrary, there is in the style of Sannazaro's Latin a sense that only words of a certain dignity will be admitted, and it is hard to miss the implication that this stylistic selectivity or exclusivity has a moral counterpart.

The translation I gave above is, I know, abjectly unhelpful. Where the Latin is elegant and strikingly succinct, the translation is clumsy and wordy, requiring over half again as many words as the original. But perhaps even in the translation it will be apparent that we have here the same inconsistency between her speech and her character that was noted in an earlier passage above. It is not just that the passage violates the canons of modern novelistic realism, in which poor country girls need to talk like poor country girls and not like the Prince of Poets. After all, if it is true that Sannazaro is not Ovid, it is equally true that he is not a modern novelist. But this passage does violate the canons of ancient decorum as found in the major genres (epic, tragedy, comedy) and described by Erich Auerbach, in which persons of low station must be presented as comic, or at least not taken very seriously.

There is also another kind of inconsistency or inconcinnity between the style and the Biblical authority of the background text, the Magnificat. The impulse to full expression that informs this passage is, after all, the antithesis of Biblical style, as Auerbach and others describe it. Auerbach says in *Mimesis:*

> The total content of the sacred writings was placed in an exegetic context which often removed the thing told very far from its sensory base, in that the reader or listener was forced to turn his attention away from the sensory occurrence and toward its meaning.[26]

If we can grant that the stylistic austerity of the original scriptural texts is a matter of profound consequence, then the modern impulse toward concretizing the narratives in retelling that

is exhibited in Neo-Latin by Sannazaro and in the vernacular
by Milton, is a matter of profound consequence, too. Later in
Mimesis Auerbach states:

> The more cultivated in the antique sense of the term, the
> more deeply imbued with antique culture the writers of the
> patristic period were, the more imperatively did they feel
> the need for casting the content of Christianity in a mold
> which should be not a mere translation but an assimilation
> to their own tradition of perception and expression.[27]

This observation could be applied to the Renaissance human-
ists as well; but neither Auerbach nor I think that it eliminates
the tension in the texts that we are interpreting. "In such a
passage . . . , one clearly recognizes the struggle in which the
two worlds were engaged in matters of language as well as
in matters of fact."[28] Auerbach is speaking about Augustine's
City of God, but his words fit our present context, too. Fantazzi
criticizes a four-line passage in the final edition:[29]

> Cumque caput fuerit tantorumque una malorum
> foemina principium lacrimasque et funera terris
> intulerit: nunc auxilium ferat ipsa modumque
> qua licet afflictis imponat foemina rebus.
>
> (1.51–54)

> (And since a single woman was the source and beginning
> of such great evils and brought weeping and death to
> the earth, now a woman likewise ["ipsa"] should bring
> help and, wherever possible, set a limit to our troubles.)

Fantazzi prefers the earlier version:

> cum fuerit tantorum sola malorum
> foemina principium, reparet quoque foemina damnum.

> (Since a single woman was the beginning of such great
> evils, a woman also should repair the damage.)

One perhaps can agree with Fantazzi's judgment in terms of
just these two passages. But what we approve in the earlier pair
of lines is its almost Biblical simplicity—and this was exactly
what Sannazaro was trying to avoid. After all, this is the version that Sannazaro thought he had improved on.

And yet I would distinguish the problem as it appears in
Sannazaro from its appearances in the vernacular. If we cannot go to our own modern literature, or to the classics, or to
the Bible, to find the criteria by which such a passage can be
judged, I do not think that we can go to the vernacular literature of the Renaissance either, unfortunately. Of course, something of this inconsistency is frequently found in the vernacular; it is the spirit of Christian humanism, we like to say. But
there is something very peculiar about Neo-Latin literature
and its *manner of meaning* that is not paralleled in the vernacu-
lars. I first became aware of this peculiarity some years ago
when I made a verse translation of one of Mantuan's eclogues.
In the brief preface to the published translation, I felt bound
to confess that "there is something peculiarly wrongheaded
about translating Neo-Latin poetry," and I went on to explain:

> Translating Vergil makes sense in a way translating Man-
> tuan, or any other Neo-Latin poet, does not. Vergil doubt-
> less did everything he could to elevate his language and
> purify it of the ephemera of daily talk, but in this effort he
> is not to be distinguished from Dante, Ronsard, or Milton:
> Latin was his native tongue. The Neo-Latin poet, on the
> other hand, deliberately eschewed the vernacular in favor
> of a language which was artificial, antique, and elitist. Neo-
> Latin poetry, then, is in a sense already a translation, but in

reverse. Instead of accommodating an ancient idiom to his own experience, by classicizing or "ennobling" the vernacular, the Neo-Latin poet has accommodated his experience to the ancient idiom. In other words, the idiom is the more important consideration. Consequently, a translation of a Neo-Latin poem must deny the continuity of literary and linguistic tradition which it was the essence of the original to affirm. How would one "translate" into modern English Spenser's Chaucerian idiom or T. S. Eliot's French poems?[30]

It must be realized that the same words, a verse of poetry, for example, written once by Vergil and written again by Vida or Sannazaro, will *not* have the same meaning. It is not that the words have changed their meanings, for the Neo-Latinist tries as hard to use the words in exactly the way in which they were or would have been used by Vergil and Cicero. The high degree of their success is what makes it possible for most of us to read Neo-Latin without the assistance of a Neo-Latin dictionary.[31] It is, rather, the context or conditions of utterance that have changed radically. When Vergil wrote, "Vltima Cumaei uenit iam carminis aetas" (*Eclogue* 4.4), it had a denotative meaning and a connotative meaning, both perfectly "natural." When Sannazaro wrote the very same line as part of *De Partu Virginis* (3.200), the denotative meaning remained the same as Vergil's, but the connotative meaning became utterly different, and in this case the latter threatens to overwhelm the former.

The untranslatability of Neo-Latin is not just a consequence of the irreproducible artificiality of the language itself. It is also true that the classical linguistic and stylistic structures of Neo-Latin are—or theory suggests that they must be—radically incompatible with modern, even early modern, experi-

ence. It is possible, if you have both the talent and the train-
ing, to write a trio sonata in the musical idiom of J. S. Bach;
you may even be able to fool somebody into thinking that it
is an original. E. K. Rand was prompted to make this now-
familiar claim about Milton's *Elegia Quinta:* "Really if Milton
had written it on musty parchment and had somebody discover it, the Classical pundits of his day would have proved beyond question by all the tests of scholarship that a lost work of
Ovid had come to light."[32] But your pseudo-Bach trio sonata
is *not* the genuine article; or at a minimum you will find it
almost impossible to express in Bach's idiom anything peculiar to contemporary experience. The musical example is most
instructive. Look at how such composers as Stravinsky, Pro-
koviev, Ralph Vaughan Williams, and Hindemith "translate"
early music into modern terms. The success of Milton's ap-
proximation of the antique in the *Elegia Quinta* surely has a lot
to do with the fact that the poem has no peculiarly modern
material in it. It would be hard to explain how it is a modern
poem nonetheless—if indeed it is—because it is very hard for
us to appreciate the tone of such a work or the effect produced
in the seventeenth century by it. And this is the very difficulty
we encounter in reading Sannazaro.

Jerome's Vulgate version is clearly a translation; what about
Sannazaro's? Perhaps we should borrow the words of Auerbach quoted above and say that it is "not a mere translation but
an assimilation to [his] own tradition of perception and expression." And yet the language remains the same. That Sannazaro
knew the original Greek seems likely, but both for him and
his audience the Vulgate version would be more familiar and
therefore more likely to resonate behind his Neo-Latin lines.
Are we to conclude that for the Neo-Latin poet, Latin was the
fullest and most "natural" mode of "perception and expres-

sion," while for his contemporaries writing in the vernacular, it was not?

Sannazaro's style is indeed more Vergilian than Ovidian in its frequent and artful enjambment, in the relative frequency of fifth-foot spondees, and in the fondness that it exhibits for larger or more elaborate periods than Ovid is inclined to produce regularly. But it is not the epic but the bucolic Vergil that Sannazaro is emulating, and in this stylistic fact lies, I think, the key to the problems that were outlined above. There is in classical pastoral, after all, something like the tension between style and character that we have found in *De Partu Virginis:* Vergil's shepherds, at least, speak with an elegance and grace that is not undone by the occasional archaism or odd form.[33] Even Auerbach recognized the peculiarity of pastoral style, but he dismissed it:

> There are, it is true, some transitional forms in bucolic and amatory poetry, but on the whole the rule of the separation of styles . . . remains inviolable.[34]

To dismiss it was a mistake: pastoral is, in fact, the genre through which the Renaissance finds its entrée into the world of classical poetry.

The appropriateness of this is worth noting. W. R. Johnson writes about Vergil's pastorals with insight:

> Virgil chose to interpret his experience and his sensibility by means of the genre least suited to them. Pastoral form, at least as Theocritus developed it and perfected it, cannot order this content. Thus, in Virgil's *Eclogues,* disintegrating pastoral form mirrors disintegrating religious content . . . , and thus the haunting multiple ironies of failed cosmos, failed refuge, failed identity, and failed poetry begin their

intricate, endlessly beautiful, endlessly mournful configura-
tions. . . . Virgil had misunderstood Theocritus's pastorals
from the beginning, and as his own desperations prolifer-
ated, he kept creating ironic surface beauties to mask what
he took to be emptiness—the emptiness, as he thought,
of Theocritus and the emptiness (*Geistlosigkeit*) of his own
world.[35]

Sannazaro was doing something similar and more radical. I
have suggested already that he was translating himself back
into the Vergilian world of language, but I suggest only now
what I take to have been his motive: he wished to "mask the
emptiness" both of his beloved models and of his own world.

Translation in Reverse

In view of the various inevitable deficiencies of a Neo-Latin
Paradise Lost that have been sketched above, you have to wonder what in the world motivated William Dobson. Earlier
translators such as Hog had probably been sufficiently moved
by a desire to make Milton's masterpiece more accessible to
continental readers ignorant of English.[36] Later translators,
especially those attempting only a part of the poem, may have
wanted chiefly to display their talent for Latin versifying. Both
of these may have been contributory motives in Dobson's case,
too, but I suspect yet a third motive, one that links him with
great original poets in Neo-Latin. Indeed, Dobson was not an
original poet; he was a translator. But unlike other translators,
Dryden, for example, or Dobson's contemporary Christopher
Pitt, he was translating backward: from his own world *back
toward Vergil's*. I submit that Petrarch, Sannazaro, Vida, Poli-
tian, Buchanan, and the young Milton, even in their original
Neo-Latin verse were, translators, too. Sannazaro, instead of

translating forwards from the New Testament into his own day, was starting in his Christian world and trying to go back. In fact, it seems to me that the Biblical passage is just a stop along the way toward the real goal, which is the classical world of Vergil. He differs from Dobson chiefly in that his translation is its own original. This idea is less paradoxical in these times of laser printers than it may have been previously.

In the fourth of his first series of essays on *Paradise Lost* in *The Spectator,* Joseph Addison observed that

> the works of ancient authors, which are written in dead languages, have a great advantage over those which are written in languages that are now spoken. Were there any mean phrases or idioms in Virgil and Homer, they would not shock the ear of the most delicate modern reader so much as they would have done that of an old Greek or Roman, because we never hear them pronounced in our streets, or in ordinary conversation. (*Spectator,* no. 285 [26 January 1712])

By writing in Neo-Latin, the modern poet sought to obtain for himself the same advantage, except that the ephemera to be purged were those of the modern rather than the ancient world. I suppose that if they thought in this way at all about what they were doing, the original Neo-Latinists, prose writers as well as poets, would have described it as a way of testing modern experience against the standards of antique perfection. I believe that this was also William Dobson's ultimate motive in translating *Paradise Lost.* It was basically a critical act, an attempt to distill Milton's classical quintessence. In its queer way it is a remarkable achievement. On the other hand, from Dobson's poem you would never guess that it had been *Milton's* aim to test the humane and mortal wisdom of classical litera-

ture against the divine and undying standards revealed in the
Bible. Dobson has undercut Milton's strategy of engagement,
which depends on the critical allusion, and as a consequence,
Paradise Lost's provocative commerce with the ancient classics
has been traduced. It should be a lesson to us all.

The Vergilian Design of *Paradise Lost* and the Poem's Earlier Versions

The Number of Books in *Paradise Lost* is equal to those of the *Aeneid*. Our Author in his First Edition had divided his Poem into ten Books, but afterwards broke the Seventh and the Eleventh each of them into two different Books, by the Help of some small Additions. This second Division was made with great Judgment, as any one may see who will be at pains of examining it. It was not done for the sake of such a Chimerical Beauty as that of resembling *Virgil* in this Particular, but for the more just and regular Disposition of this great Work.

—Joseph Addison, *The Spectator*

This is Addison, one of Milton's fittest readers, remarking upon the numerical analogy to Vergil, only to dismiss it. I think that Addison is wrong, and I shall attempt presently to demonstrate that the redivision of *Paradise Lost* into twelve books was made to clarify the design of the poem, which Milton regarded not as a "Chimerical Beauty," but as an aspect of his very deliberate challenge to the master of pagan poetry. I know that I am wading into a dangerous swamp here. But the fact that the poem was published originally in ten books needs explanation. And while that is being examined, a reader who wishes

to see in the twelve books a truly epical design may wish to
consider another inconvenient fact as well: that Milton's subject—the Fall of Adam and Eve—was originally chosen with
an eye to the composition of a tragic drama, rather than an
epic. I offer this appendix in order to avoid giving the impression that, in chapter 3 above, I was arguing in blithe disregard
of certain literary historical unpleasantries.

Several drafts of the early plan for a drama on the Fall are
preserved in the so-called Trinity manuscript and reveal a disposition of the material that is in most respects unlike that
of the epic we read today. This project appears to have been
abandoned at the outbreak of the Civil War in 1642. The subject lay fallow in Milton's imagination for about fifteen years
before he returned to it, now with the epic genre in mind.[1]
This knowledge of Milton's early dramatic design is of no more
necessary consequence to the interpretation of the final poem
than is the knowledge that his original epic topic had been
King Arthur and the Knights of the Round Table.[2] It appears,
however, to have encouraged a search—especially in this century—for dramatic structure in *Paradise Lost*, and this search
seems to have attenuated or compromised the epic design of
the poem.[3] So Helen Gardner, having identified an unresolved
contradiction in *Paradise Lost* between the dramatic treatment
of Satan and the requirements of epic structure, suggests that
this contradiction has its origin in Milton's change of mind
about the genre of *Paradise Lost*. She describes Milton, in his
development of Satan's character, as "what we loosely call an
Elizabethan, sacrificing simplicity of effect and strength of design to imaginative opportunity; creating the last great tragic
figure in our literature and destroying the unity of his poem
in doing so."[4]

It cannot be denied that aspects of the structure of *Paradise
Lost* may be described by the word *dramatic*, in the sense of re-

sembling or suggesting a drama, but not in the sense of *being*
one. The same has been said with even greater justness about
the *Aeneid*, especially book 4, which—in its concentration on
a single limited action and a few characters, the rhetorical ex-
changes of speeches, and, especially, the tragic portrayal of its
heroine—has called Euripides to the minds of many readers.
Students of the English theater will recall that Marlowe did
in fact translate Dido's tragedy to the stage and that Purcell
made an opera of it. But with regard to Milton, because of the
knowledge of the "original"—that is, preoriginal—dramatic
design, the vitality of this critical metaphor has been enhanced
much beyond what it would have been had the earlier design
consented to a respectable interment with its author.

Now the question of whether the poem's design is dramatic,
rather than epic, is related to the problem of the redivision
of the books. The 1667 poem differed from the twelve-book
second edition of 1674 in only two simple respects—but what
momentous effect they have had upon interpretation! The
original books 7 and 10 were divided in two, producing the
present books 7–8 and 11–12. (The intervening books were
renumbered accordingly.) Secondly, while not a single line was
excised in the redivision, fifteen lines were added, mainly to
smooth transitions: three new lines were worked in at 5.636–
39; three were added to the opening of the new book 8; in
book 11, three lines were inserted at lines 485–87, and one was
worked in at lines 551–52; and five new lines were added at
the opening of the new book 12.[5] The fact that the substance
of the poem was virtually unaltered confines the critical consequences of the redivision to two rather abstract matters: the
significance of the altered interrelation of the books, and the
possible literary significance of the numbers ten and twelve.

While some critics have insisted upon the presence of a dramatic pattern even in the second edition, others have argued

that the structure of the first was dramatic in ways that the second was not.[6] Satan was the tragic hero of this dramatic structure, presenting a figure like Aeschylus' Prometheus in some respects and like Shakespeare's Macbeth in others. According to this hypothesis, the ten books divide naturally into five two-book "acts." The figure of Satan initially seems to be the center of the poet's interest, since the action begins with him and because the first two-thirds of the poem—by count of books—were occupied with his machinations (books 1 through 6). This appearance of Satan's centrality seems to be confirmed in the crucial fourth act, where the grouping of books (present 7 and 8 followed by present 9) suggests that Satan the protagonist has accomplished his revenge, marring God's creation by bringing about the Fall of Man. This analysis concludes that it was to correct these misleading emphases that Milton redivided the poem into twelve books—although the adherents of this hypothesis seem to be divided as to whether the redivision was successful.[7]

On the other hand, it has been observed that the idea of two-book acts works best for the first four books and rather less well thereafter. In particular, the prologue to book 8 (now book 9) would have clumsily interrupted the putative act four.[8] And the first edition is by no means unequivocally more tragic than the second. After all, the first edition no less than the second had aspired to justify the ways of God to humans and to this end marshaled the very same poetry (less fifteen lines) that in the second edition seems to throw emphasis upon the *felix culpa* theme:

> O goodness infinite, goodness immense!
> That all this good of evil shall produce,
> And evil turn to good.
>
> (12.469–71)

In particular, the numerological symbolism of the first edition is more manifestly Christian than that of the second. The number ten was traditionally a symbol of divine perfection. Furthermore, the natural groupings of books have been thought by some scholars to be patterned upon the "divine tetrachys," a sequence of the numbers one through four, whose sum is ten. The invocations in the original edition's books 1, 3, 7, and 8 divide the poem into groups of two, four, one, and three books apiece.[9] Even without the numerological argument (which does not interest me personally), this grouping of the books has more to recommend it than the five-act hypothesis, as it is based on the striking and undeniable evidence of the prologues. And the emphases of this grouping of the book are upon the good that God brings out of evil. This Christological analysis of the division into ten books is especially important because it is more likely to represent Milton's conscious intention than the hypothesis of dramatic structure.

The second edition emphasizes the triumph of good over evil. When the original book 10 was divided into present books 11 and 12, these were among the lines prefixed to book 12 to signal the thematic transition:

> As one who in his journey bates at noon,
> Though bent on speed, so here the archangel paused
> Betwixt the world destroyed and world restored.
>
> (12.1–3)

That is, Michael's account of mankind's sinfulness, culminating in the story of the Flood, now sits by itself in book 11, and is counterbalanced by the history of God's salvific involvement with Israel in book 12, which culminates in the arrival of the Redeemer near the end of the poem. This small, almost mechanical change in the structure makes a significant differ-

ence in the way that the narrative is perceived. The following
lines were in the first edition, too, but in the second edition
their hopefulness seems more justifiable:

> then wilt thou not be loath
> To leave this Paradise, but shalt possess
> A paradise within thee, happier far.
>
> (12.585–87)

Something similar is accomplished by the redivision of the
poem into two, more clearly balanced halves: the first concerned with Satan and concluding with his expulsion from
Heaven; the second concerned with the world and humankind, centering indeed upon the Fall, but framing it with the
account of Creation in 7 and the promise of redemption in 12.
The contrast between the halves, like that between books 11
and 12, is the contrast between the destructive power of evil
and the creative (and restorative) powers of God.

As suggested above, the division of the poem into two halves
has another motive as well: it is part of Milton's Vergilian design. And there is clear evidence that this design was already
intended in the first edition. First, the claim "Half yet remains
unsung" (7.21, compare with *Aeneid* 7.45), while inaccurate in
terms of books, is accurate in terms of total lines and pages.[10]
Another aspect of the first edition's disposition of material
that deserves notice is the excessive length of books 7 and 10,
especially the latter. The longest book in the poem as we have
it now is 9, with 1189 lines. The 1667 book 7, with 1289 lines,
was exactly one hundred lines longer; and the 1667 book 10,
with 1546 lines, was over 350 lines longer. Considering the
length of these books and the ease with which their bisection
was accomplished, along with the evidence of Milton's attention to the proportions of the poem, it is difficult to suppress

the suspicion that the possibility of a division into twelve books had occurred to Milton even *before* the first edition.[11]

Either the redivision into twelve books represents a change of mind, implying that Milton had in some way not fully understood what he was doing in 1667, or it represents more clearly a design that had already been intended in the first edition, but that had somehow been confused by the division into ten books. The former alternative has commonly been the only one considered by those interested in this problem, who have been too intent upon explaining the first edition fully before turning to the second. (So Louis L. Martz, employing an ingenuity born of desperation, explains the ten-book edition by reference to Camoëns's *Lusiad*.[12]) Approached this way, the redivision can hardly avoid looking like an afterthought. Joseph Summers makes a nice distinction when he says, "The publication of the poem in twelve books seems to have been the result of a change in Milton's perception of what he had already made, rather than of a decision to make something new."[13] It seems preposterous to suppose that Milton would have abandoned a splendid dramatic structure, cooked up out of Castelvetro, in order simply to remind people that he was also writing an epic, or even to make it easier to divide the poem into two halves and three thirds.

Instead of looking upon the second edition as a perfunctory repackaging of the same goods, then, it seems to make more sense to regard it as the *telos* toward which Milton had been striving all along and to look upon the double design of the first edition as an ambitious experiment that failed. Milton from the very beginning built into the poem a moderately complex Vergilian design, and he intended in the first edition to counterpoint that design against the Christian number symbolism of the book divisions. At various points throughout this book but especially in the last chapter, I argue that this sort of counterpoint was essential to his style, which is at once classical and Biblical. I believe that he originally hoped for something similar in the form of the poem. But there the counterpoint failed, not exactly because its emphases were misleading, but because one voice ended up drowning out the other. Milton's response was to jettison the Christian number symbolism, which had always been less important than the Vergilian structural pattern according to which the poem had been constructed episode by episode. The outcome was a clearer antinomy between classical form and Biblical content—what I believe Milton had been aiming at all along.[14]

My presentation of these matters is admittedly somewhat circular. The exposition of Vergilian patterns in chapter 3 relies upon my belief that the twelve-book design was deliberate, while that belief is strengthened by the recognition of the Vergilian patterns. This is, however, not an instance of logical circularity or tautology, but of hermeneutic circularity. I refer, of course, to the "hermeneutic circle," that conundrum about parts and wholes that theorists have articulated to characterize the mystery of understanding.

Notes

Introduction

1. Harding, *Club of Hercules*, p. 134.

2. Blessington, *"Paradise Lost" and the Classical Epic*, pp. xi, 1.

3. Harding, *Club of Hercules*, p. 45.

4. Or his less Greek. Harding, making a point about the opening of the *Odyssey* (*Club of Hercules*, p. 27), misidentifies the poem's first word, ἄνδρα, which he wrongly takes to be a form of ἄνθρωπος. (It is from the very different word ἀνήρ.) Harding's two books contain numerous errors of this sort.

5. Blessington, *"Paradise Lost" and the Classical Epic*, p. 49.

6. W. R. Johnson, Preface to *Momentary Monsters*, p. ix.

7. DuRocher, *Milton and Ovid,* p. 19.

8. DuRocher's procedure is, in fact, not ahistorical. He says on the very next page of his Introduction, "Because Ovid's *Metamorphoses* has been interpreted in various ways throughout history, we need to know how its interpeters before Milton prepared him to read it" (*Milton and Ovid*, p. 20).

9. Even though these features have received vastly more critical attention in this century than the details of verbal allusion, they have not always been well handled. However, since I will have scant need to call upon it for my argument here, I do wish to acknowledge one book that I find very rich, Webber's *Milton and His Epic Tradition*.

Chapter 1
Nec plura adludens: Allusion

1. See the introduction in *Complete Poems and Major Prose,* ed. Hughes, paragraph 56, pp. xlvi-xlvii, for a survey of the various sources that have been adduced for Milton's use of *light* here.

2. "Vitaque cum gemitu fugit indignata sub umbras" ("and his [*or* her] spirit with a groan fled complaining to the shades below") occurs twice: at 11.831 (of Camilla), and at 12.952, the final verse of the poem (describing Turnus).

3. Even the reliable R. D. Williams, whose compact commentary is usually the first thing I consult on the *Aeneid,* misdirects the reader to Ovid, *Met.* 13.410–11, which simply mentions Cassandra, rather than citing the proper reference to Ajax at 14.468–69.

4. DuRocher, *Milton and Ovid,* p. 17, speaks of "the overwhelming quantity of Ovidian analogues and allusions" in the modern commentaries of Hughes, Bush, and Fowler, but this suggests only that DuRocher is easily overwhelmed. The number of poetic references to Ovid claimed even in Fowler, who is most thorough, is quite small, especially when the modern commentaries are compared to those of Newton and Todd.

5. Harding distinguishes between three kinds of "open borrowings": "the direct quotation, the metaphor or simile, and the verbal echo" (*Club of Hercules,* p. 91). His distinctions are carelessly made. He speaks of "direct quotation" and "translation" interchangeably, without recognizing that every reference to classical literature depends upon translation: there is not a single quotation of Vergil in *Paradise Lost.* Metaphoric borrowings are illustrated with one example that turns out not to be a metaphor at all, but a simile ("The sun, as from Thyestean banquet, turned," 10.688; see Harding, p. 95). And in any case he does not justify his designation of "metaphor and simile" as a separate category in view of the obvious possibility that a simile may be a "direct quotation" or "verbal echo." But these are minor problems. There are two major faults in Harding's discussion. First, while he attempts to distinguish between the varieties of "open bor-

rowing," he fails to suggest any distinctions among the major terms of his critical vocabulary: *allusion, imitation, reworking, translation, influence,* and *borrowing* itself. He appears at times to use these terms indifferently. Second, such distinctions as he does make are insensitive to the crucial difference between creative practice (the realm of *influence, background*) and critical consequence (the realm of *allusion*).

6. Harding, *Club of Hercules,* p. 92, implies that the fact that the phrase is spoken by one of the fallen angels is an indication of Milton's skillful strategy to discredit the classics. But the principle of decorum, which Harding also mentions (p. 110), is sufficient to explain why Milton did not place the phrase in the mouth of Gabriel or the Son.

7. Quoted by Harding, *Club of Hercules,* p. 109.

8. Hollander, *Figure of Echo,* p. ix.

9. Cf. also Catullus 62.39–42, *Aeneid* 11.68–71.

10. Conte, *Rhetoric of Imitation,* pp. 88–91.

11. See Hollander's remarks, *Figure of Echo,* pp. 110–11, on echoes in Milton and Tennyson of a simile in Vergil. The conservatism of the epic tradition is particularly apparent in a poet's similes, and it may be that they are among the most common *loci* of echo.

12. Willey, *Seventeenth Century Background,* p. 70.

13. I doubt that it strengthens the allusive link to do so, but "ora tenebant" can also be taken to mean "kept quiet"; see *Aeneid of Virgil,* ed. R. D. Williams.

14. Cf. Spenser, *Faerie Queene* 1.11.8.

15. Gordon Williams's comments on Milton's debt to Vergil are worth looking at (*Tradition and Originality,* p. 643).

16. Adams, *Milton and the Modern Critics,* p. 145. This one chapter, "Milton's Reading," contains more good sense than can be found in most books on the subject.

17. Conte observes that Homer himself was charged with stealing from Orpheus; see Conte, *Rhetoric of Imitation,* p. 77, and references cited there.

18. Eliot, *Selected Essays,* p. 182. It is not implausible that Eliot may here be consciously echoing Vergil.

19. Conte, *Rhetoric of Imitation,* p. 30, and on the same page, n. 13.

20. Aristotle acknowledges that rhetorical argumentation is often based on contingent propositions or probabilities, so that enthymemes are not dialectically compelling even after the missing premises have been supplied. See Lanham's brief but incisive description of the term *enthymeme* in the *Handlist of Rhetorical Terms*, p. 41.

21. See Quintilian, *Institutio Oratoria* 5.10.1–3 and 5.10.1–4.

22. George Kennedy notes that the *Pro Ligario* is "exceedingly clever" and says, "The speech throughout is ironic" (*Art of Rhetoric in the Roman World*, pp. 262–63).

23. Lyne, *Further Voices*, p. 103. The weakness of many of the allegedly allusive links that Lyne presents tells against his assertion.

24. Knauer, *Die "Aeneis" und Homer*, comments more sensibly on Vergil's *Detailimitationen:* "bis auf bestimmte, wohl begründete Ausnahmen lässt sich nicht unbedingt eine innere Beziehung zwischen dem homerischen und vergilischen Zusammenhang erkennen" (p. 53).

25. Camps, *Introduction to Virgil's "Aeneid*," p. 9.

Chapter 2
Descende caelo: Thought

1. The major exponent of this view has been John M. Steadman, most notably in *Milton and the Renaissance Hero*. Though not universal, the view is widely repeated, even taken for granted, and seldom challenged.

2. Gallagher, "*Paradise Lost* and the Greek Theogony."

3. But see Revard's article, "Milton's Muse and the Daughters of Memory," which is more sensitive to the irony of Milton's "rejection" of the classical Muse than is the article by Gallagher, cited above, which appears in the same issue of *English Literary Renaissance;* see especially Revard, pp. 432–34. My main complaint with her piece is simply that she fails to pursue the matter to the point where it becomes really interesting. She is more concerned with the sources of Milton's Muse-lore than with his pregnant references to Hesiod's text.

4. Behind Vergil's lines lie those of Lucretius describing Ennius

as the poet "qui primus amoeno / detulit ex Helicone perenni fronde coronam" (1.117–18: "who first brought down from pleasant Helicon a crown with undying leaves"). Significantly, however, while Lucretius' lines look backward to another's accomplishment, Vergil's lines look forward to what he hopes for himself. Later, similar declarations of intent will be made by many others, notably by Dante, at the end of the *Vita Nuova*, and Milton, who made something of a career of these promises: cf. *Mansus* 78–79, *Epitaphium Damonis* 168–69 (which alludes to the lines quoted here from the *Georgics*), and in prose, the promise to "leave something so written to aftertimes, as they should not willingly let it die" (*Reason of Church Government*, preface to book 2).

5. Evidently Gallagher, "*Paradise Lost* and the Greek Theogony," pp. 128–29, thinks "the Aonian mount" and Olympus are one and the same.

6. See West's commentary upon the *Theogony*, p. 152.

7. See, among others, Minton, "Homer's Invocations of the Muses."

8. Pindar speaks of the Muses often and with real fervor, but his remarks are scattered and brief; see especially the fragments quoted by Bowra, *Pindar*, chap. 1, pp. 6, 8, and 33. Callimachus in the *Aitia* links his encounter with the Muses to Hesiod's; see the Loeb edition of Callimachus' fragments, ed. Trypanis, pp. 8–9 and 84–87. The most important Latin *loci* for Milton are Vergil, *Georgics* 2.475–76 (alluded to in the prologues to *Paradise Lost* 3 and 9), and Horace, *Odes* 3.4 (cf. *Paradise Lost* 7's prologue). Noteworthy but inapposite to Milton's concerns are Lucretius 1.922–23 and Propertius 3.3. Further references will be found in West, pp. 158–61.

9. Cf. Revard, "Milton's Muse," p. 437.

10. Pucci, *Hesiod and the Language of Poetry*, pp. 30–31. Note that separating oneself from the tradition in this way is quite different from what is done by those poets who reject the Muses altogether; see Curtius, *European Literature and the Latin Middle Ages*, pp. 233, 235; and cf. Revard's important point that Milton does not have to invoke

a Muse at all ("Milton's Muse," p. 432). Gadamer notes in "Composition and Interpretation," pp. 72–73, that the cryptic lines of the Muses about truth and falsehood in Hesiod's prologue should not be taken as a criticism of the Homeric poems: they mean instead that poetry always contains an element of both truth and falsehood. He says, in essay 6 of the same volume, "On the contribution of poetry to the search for truth," p. 105, that formerly the truth claims of poetry, especially those of the early epic, went unchallenged. This should be set alongside his reading of the lines from Hesiod's Muses. Gadamer observes that "we no longer show the same naive readiness to learn that was characteristic of earlier times."

11. The original title page of *Noble Numbers* is reproduced in L. C. Martin's edition of Herrick, p. 337.

12. Hesiod himself mentions having won a prize in a poetic competition, but he does not name his opponent: *Works and Days* 654–59.

13. The first-person verb in Vergil's opening, "Arma uirumque cano," is admittedly a bit bold, and elsewhere Vergil's narrative voice intrudes more personally and more insistently than even Milton's. Vergil's voice is truly personal and invites empathy—Brooks Otis dubbed it the "subjective style"—while Milton's is beyond personalism: idiosyncratic, antagonistic, prophetic.

14. For a convenient review of prior work, see Sundell, "Singer and His Song."

15. Cf. the reference at the beginning of the seventh *Prolusion* to the "divine sleep of Hesiod," alluding to the nocturnal epiphany of the Muses at the beginning of the *Theogony;* the student orator implies that this "sleep" symbolizes in fact, the studies that Hesiod had pursued (*Works of John Milton,* ed. Patterson, 12.248).

16. Kerrigan, *Prophetic Milton,* p. 15.

17. Pucci, *Hesiod and the Language of Poetry,* pp. 31–33.

18. The *editio princeps* of Hesiod, ed. Demetrius Chalcondyles (Milan, ca. 1480), contained only the *Works and Days.* The *Theogony* was first printed by Aldus (Venice, 1495), although a Latin verse translation of it by Boninus Mombritius of Milan had been in print

since 1474. In all the Renaissance editions I have examined, the notes to the *Works and Days* are more extensive than those to the *Theogony*.

19. For a survey of these precedents (including some attention to Hesiod), see Revard, *War in Heaven*, pp. 148–52, 192–94; and Hughes, "Milton's Celestial Battle and the Theogonies," pp. 196–219.

20. See Blessington, *"Pardise Lost" and the Classical Epic*, pp. 8–14; and Harding, *Club of Hercules*, pp. 108–9.

21. See Hughes's note in *Complete Poems and Major Prose*, at *Paradise Lost* 1.50.

22. In the copy of Schrevelius's Hesiod (London, 1659) available on microfilm, STC 1605, an asterisk marks these lines, and in the bottom margin of the page one may read in English the handwritten note: "A distance, if my calculation is correct, of about 1,846,870,800 miles."

23. Cf. the similar overgoing of Homer (*Iliad* 8.16) and Vergil (*Aeneid* 6.577–79) at *Paradise Lost* 1.73–74 (distance from heaven to hell).

24. Some commentators refer *Paradise Lost* 2.650–53 (Sin: woman above, serpent below) to *Theogony* 298–300 (Echidna), but cf., among others, Ovid, *Metamorphoses* 14.40–74 (Scylla), and Spenser, *Fairie Queene* 1.1.14 (Error).

25. Thyer, in *Poetical Works of John Milton*, ed. Todd, refers *Paradise Lost* 6.386, "the battle swerv'd," to *Theogony* 711, "the battle inclined" (ἐκλίνθη δέ μάχη), but the contexts are not analogous.

26. The occasional hints of concomitant parallels with the other celestial rebellions in ancient myth, those of the giants (*Paradise Lost* 7.605) and Typhon (1.199), invariably link these monsters with the rebel angels; on these see Harding, *Milton and the Renaissance Ovid*, pp. 85–86; and Labriola, "Titans and the Giants."

27. Even Harding, *Club of Hercules*, affirms the absolute primacy of Homer and Vergil. Hesiod and Ovid, whose importance for Milton has recently received fresh attention, are within the epic tradition as classical scholars (in Milton's day, as in our own) have understood it. See Colie, *Resources of Kind,* especially pp. 119–22, for a liberat-

ing essay on the mixed genre in the Renaissance. Lewalski's *"Paradise Lost" and the Rhetoric of Literary Forms* is in some ways a heavier-handed rehearsal of a similar argument; the same author's much briefer essay, "Genres of *Paradise Lost*," covers much of the same ground.

28. Following T. E. Page, Kenneth Quinn, in his commentary on the *Odes*, at 3.4.20, translates, "though yet too young to speak, divinely inspired," and notes that this is an oxymoron. "Animosus," however, ordinarily means "courageous"; see *Oxford Latin Dictionary*, s.v. "animosus." I regard the line as deliberately ambiguous.

29. I am indebted to the thorough and intelligent reading of the ode by Commager, *Odes of Horace*, pp. 194–209.

30. This numerical analogy would not, of course, have been so apparent in the 1667 first edition of *Paradise Lost* in ten books. I am not among those who believe that the 1674 redivision was an afterthought; see my discussion in the appendix; even so, I need not press the structural homology.

31. For example, the final lines of *Orlando Furioso* and *Paradise Lost* 4 allude to the last line of the *Aeneid;* the openings of *The Faerie Queene* and *Paradise Regained* allude to the well-known variant opening of the *Aeneid* ("Ille ego qui quondam"); the first lines of canto 4 of *The Rape of the Lock* and *The Dunciad* 2 allude to the first lines of the like-numbered books of the *Aeneid*. Examples could easily be multiplied. On the use of an allusion in the opening lines, I know of nothing better than the remarks of Conte, who calls it "the quintessential literary act" (*Rhetoric of Imitation*, pp. 69–79).

32. "Arma" (which Servius glosses as a figure for "bella") is a reference to the theme of the *Iliad;* but Vergil's verb "cano" is the same as the imperative ἀεῖδε, *Iliad* 1.1. "Virum" translates ἄνδρα, the first word of the *Odyssey*. Conte observes, moreover, that the *Aeneid*'s "arma uirumque" simultaneously signals Vergil's intention to imitate Ennius as well as Homer (*Rhetoric of Imitation*, pp. 70–73). Vergil even refers to himself by first lines repeatedly. *Eclogue* 5.86–87 contain quotations referring to the openings of *Eclogues* 2 and 3 respectively; and the final line of the *Georgics* alludes to the first line of the *Eclogues*.

Pope imitates this ornament, alluding in the final line of *Windsor Forest* to the first line of his own *Pastorals*.

33. Compare, for example, the openings of the Cleopatra ode (1.37), "Nunc est bibendum," with Alcaeus' νῦν χρῆ μεθύσθην (fragment 332 in vol. 1 of Campbell, *Greek Lyric*); the opening of *Odes* 1.9 with Alcaeus' fragment 338, of 1.18 with Alcaeus' fragment 342, and of 1.12 with Pindar's *Olympian* 2.2.

34. Or so Tacitus seemed to view the establishment of the Principate; see *Annales* 1.1. Milton seems to have been sympathetic with Tacitus' interpretation of the history of the two first centuries.

35. In the great odes about his vocation besides 3.14, Horace names Euterpe and Polyhymnia (both in 1.1), and Melpomene twice (3.30 and 4.3).

36. Not to mention that Milton's implication of Bacchus in the murder is directly contrary to the account of Ovid, the primary authority, in *Metamorphoses* 11 (see 67–87).

37. Ovid also plays into Milton's allusion to Horace in another way: in the *Metamorphoses*, Orpheus (book 10) sings about a revolt in Heaven, and Calliope (book 5) responds to a song about the gigantomachy sung by the Pierides.

38. I accept the identification of Bacchus with Charles II, though I see no reason why this must fix the composition of the lines in 1660; see Hughes's note and references.

39. According to Finley, "Milton and Horace," p. 50, Milton's praises of Cromwell as "chief of men" (Sonnet 10) and "patriae liberator" (*Second Defense*) call to mind Horace's praises of Augustus. But some of the titles Milton applies to Cromwell in the same context, especially "pater patriae" ("father of his country"), might suit other men, ancient or modern, equally well. It was Cicero's boast to have been acclaimed "pater patriae" by the Senate after he quashed the Catilinarian conspiracy; the Earl of Clarendon in his *History of the Rebellion* applied the title to John Hampden rather than to Cromwell.

40. Kerrigan, *Prophetic Milton*, especially chap. 3.

41. Actually Horace's background here is complicated; see the dis-

cussion of *Odes* 2.7 in *A Commentary on Horace*, ed. Nisbet and Hubbard.

42. Finley, "Milton and Horace," p. 32.

43. See Commager, chaps. 1 and 6.

44. Cf. Spenser, *"Paradise Lost:* The Anti-Epic." Spenser speaks of both "wit" and "humor"; I find the former in Milton's epic, but little of the latter. Newman, *Classical Epic Tradition*, p. 379, responds very sensibly to Milton's claim that his theme is superior to those of the classical epics: "It is a good example of a topos which the reader does well to read with a smile." A smile, not a laugh.

Chapter 3
Facilis descensus Auerno: Design

1. Quoted from *Complete Poems and Major Prose*, ed. Hughes, p. 208. Carey and Fowler unfortunately do not include this interesting little piece.

2. On this period of Milton's development see Rand, "Milton in Rustication."

3. The opening lines of *Paradise Regained*, beginning "I who erewhile the happy garden sung," do not unambiguously or pointedly refer to the false opening of the *Aeneid* ("Ille ego qui quondam . . ."). Milton knew these lines were already regarded as spurious in antiquity, and other poets before Milton had begun poems with allusions to the same lines; the most important was, of course, Spenser ("Lo! I, the man whose Muse whylome did maske"). See Carey, in *Poems of John Milton*, ed. Carey and Fowler; and cf. Anthony Low, *Georgic Revolution*, pp. 323–25, and further references there.

4. Samuel Johnson, *Lives of the English Poets*, p. 119.

5. Martz, *Milton: Poet of Exile*, n. 2, p. 331.

6. Tillyard, *English Epic*, p. 438. Tillyard claims, moreover, that the *Odyssey* is the chief model for *Paradise Lost*, but he does not argue the point.

7. Fowler is mistaken when he says (p. 456) that the note on the verse was added in the 1674 second, octavo edition. Cf. his own re-

marks on the printing history on p. 423, and the appendix to the Scolar Press facsimile of the first edition.

8. Castelvetro cites Aristarchus to support this view, which he mentions incidentally; see Gilbert, *Literary Criticism: Plato to Dryden*, p. 354.

9. Fowler's reading "Neptun's" in line 18 is obviously a rare misprint; cf. his quotation of the text at 9.10–19.

10. "Perhaps himself leaning on the precedent of Tasso's *Discourses*, Milton shamelessly pretends that war had been the literal subject of previous epics so that he can subvert it by making Satan into a mock ruler." So states Webber (*Milton and His Epic Tradition*, p. 117), but not apropos of these lines (9.27–33) in particular.

11. It had been so transformed already by the Greeks themselves; see Stanford, *Ulysses Theme*, chaps. 7, 10, and, especially, 12, "Ulysses and the Discrediting of Homer."

12. See Steadman, *Milton and the Renaissance Hero*, especially chap. 6, "The Critique of Magnanimity," and *Milton's Epic Characters*, especially chap. 13, "The Classical Hero: Satan and Ulysses."

13. Hughes glosses Milton's lines by reference to a remark attributed to Julius Caesar by Plutarch, *Life of Caesar* 11.2, to the effect that he would rather be the first man in a Spanish village than the second man in Rome. But, if anything, Caesar is himself alluding to Achilles.

14. The argument of Blessington, *"Paradise Lost" and the Classical Epic*, especially in chap. 1, would be greatly enhanced by the recognition of this allusion, but I cannot find in Blessington any mention of it.

15. See, for example, Spenser's letter to Sir Philip Sidney prefacing *The Faerie Queene*.

16. Nor does Milton refer to Horace or Hesiod by name. When Revard notes that "Milton never alludes to Hesiod directly" ("Milton's Muse," 437–38), she means *by name*, though as I said above in chap. 2, she fails to see that Milton has alluded to Hesiod's text.

17. Milton may have read "perculsus" here, as Hume cites the passage, rather than "percussus," the prevailing modern reading; but "smit" could be a translation of either word.

18. I am speaking of what C. S. Lewis in his *Preface to "Paradise Lost"* called "secondary" epic. From the fourteenth through the eighteenth centuries, when people were still writing this sort of poem, they often called it by a different name—the "heroic poem"—but they knew what it was. Dryden says in the dedicatory essay to his *Aeneis* that "A Heroic poem . . . is undoubtedly the greatest work which the soul of man is capable to perform," echoing the sentiments of the French theorist Rapin. This is epic in the sense parodied by Pope in his *Receipt for an Epic Poem,* not in one of the senses proposed by such modern theorists of the genre as Northrup Frye or even J. K. Newman, whose book *The Classical Epic Tradition* includes, among other novelties, discussions of films by Eisenstein. (I might note that the protagonist of Newman's very big book is not Vergil, but, ironically, Callimachus.) In the poetry of Statius and Claudian one can see the evidence of what might be called "tertiary" epic, in which the reader is aware that the poetry is imitating imitations, alluding to allusions; Milton would fall into this category, too. I avoid the terms *secondary* and *tertiary,* considering them not very illuminating. After all, Vergil has Apollonius, Lucretius, Ennius, and others before him. Even the *Odyssey* seems self-consciously to be playing against a countertradition that recounted the *nostos* of Agamemnon; in fact, it is beginning once again to seem plausible that the *Iliad* and *Odyssey* are the productions of a single master composer who may even have been literate! It seems to me that the epic tradition as a self-conscious fact of literary history was defined by Vergil, and that what literary works otherwise as diverse as Camoëns's *Lusiad,* Dante's *Commedia,* Tasso's *Gerusalemme Liberata,* Spenser's *Faerie Queene,* and Milton's *Paradise Lost* have in common is the homage each pays in its way to the Vergilian precedent.

19. See Barker, "Structural Pattern," p. 151; and cf. Bush, "Virgil and Milton," p. 180. For further references, see Blessington, *Paradise Lost and the Classical Epic,* chap. 4, n. 1, on p. 112. The metaphor of "movements" is borrowed from Barker.

20. Like everything in Vergil, this is much more complicated than I am making it. See Anderson, "Vergil's Second *Iliad.*"

21. The whole subject is most thoroughly treated by Knauer, *Die "Aeneis" und Homer;* "Vergil's *Aeneid* and Homer" is an English précis of his book. In *Vergil and Early Latin Poetry,* pp. 8–12, Wigodsky expresses some useful criticisms of Knauer's tendency to overvalue structural parallels.

22. See *Aeneid of Virgil,* ed. R. D. Williams, at 1.148–49.

23. Citing even part of the enormous bibliography on this relationship would be vain here. Armour's essay, "Dante's Virgil," is a good and fairly recent survey with judicious references to prior scholarship; see especially pp. 71–72.

24. Other precedents: Isaiah 34.4, *Iliad* 5.146, and cf. *Inferno* 3.112–15.

25. The interpretation of "Auerno" (6.126) is in dispute. R. D. Williams explains it as ablative of route, "by way of Avernus," which he says is much likelier here the lake around the Sibyl's caves than hell itself. Austin, on the other hand, notes that Servius regarded it as a dative and glossed it as "ad Auernum," which strikes me as absolutely necessary if the antithesis with the lines that follow is to be maintained. ("Motion toward" is regularly expressed by the accusative, but the dative is found throughout the classical period.)

26. Incidental verbal echoes such as this one do not detract from the primacy of the *structural* parallels that I am describing. Cf. the reference at *Paradise Lost* 2.528–69 to the diversion of the blessed described at *Aeneid* 6.642–59 (in the Elysian portion of the descent), or the reference at *Paradise Lost* 11.477–90 to the catalog of ills that Aeneas sees in the vestibule of hell at *Aeneid* 273–81 (in the infernal portion of the descent). Modern scholarship has on occasion shown greater concern with such things than Milton clearly did, a weakness that reflects not only an inability to distinguish between Milton's many echoes and borrowings and his few true allusions, but a more general tendency to get lost in the trees and lose sight of the forest.

27. See Taylor, *Milton's Use of Du Bartas,* pp. 112–24.

28. See Sasek, "Drama of *Paradise Lost,* Books XI and XII." Sasek seems to consider this identification of Milton's source so obvious that it need not be stated or argued as a proposition.

29. Among those who think likewise are Hume, *Annotations on Milton's "Paradise Lost,"* at 11.433; Hughes, at 357; Bush, "Virgil and Milton," p. 182; Condee, *Structure in Milton's Poetry*, p. 15; and Blessington, *"Paradise Lost" and the Classical Epic*, who says (pp. 70–71), "In the education of the hero, Michael deliberately takes over the roles of Tiresias and Anchises, the two other major prophets in classical epic. As in the scene with Raphael, Milton here chooses to follow closely the *Aeneid*." Hughes cites first *Aeneid* 6, but refers also to *Faerie Queene* 3.3.29–49, Daniel 10–13, and Du Bartas. None of these commentators, however, goes on to coordinate the parallel between Michael and Anchises with the parallel between the imitation in *Paradise Lost* 1 and 2 of the infernal part of Aeneas' descent.

30. Certain other details may lend support. The hilltop on which Michael shows Adam the visions of humankind's future (11.377–80) corresponds to the "tumulus" from which Anchises and Aeneas view the pageant of heroes (*Aeneid* 6.754–55). It seems also worth noting that Adam is in a trance (see 11.420) and Eve is asleep dreaming (see 12.595–96) during the prophetic narration of books 11 and 12, and that, similarly, on the suggestion of *Aeneid* 6.893–98 (cf. 283–84), Aeneas' vision may be a dream.

31. Many Milton critics have felt that Milton's prophetic narrative, running from 11.370 almost to the end of book 12—about 1100 lines—is regrettably out of proportion to its models. (The description of Aeneas' shield is barely over a hundred lines, *Aeneid* 8.626–728, and the prophecy of Anchises occupies not quite 150, *Aeneid* 6.752–892.) See Sasek, "Drama of *Paradise Lost*, Books XI and XII," p. 344; and Lewis, *Preface to "Paradise Lost,"* p. 129, where he accuses Milton of being "not content with following his master [i.e., Vergil] in the use of occasional prophecies, allusions, and reflections." Lewis does not refer specifically to the shield panoramas as the models for the last books.

32. See Otis, *Virgil: A Study in Civilised Poetry*, chap. 6, "The Odyssean *Aeneid*," especially pp. 291, 300–301.

33. An early reader of this book found this claim surprising, if not

incredible. It is based on a count of intertextual references observed in the early commentaries, especially Todd's second variorum, which was most thorough in this respect. Support of this observation obviously would require that I supply a table of references such as that given by Knauer in *Die "Aeneis" und Homer*. I decided not to provide such a table, mainly because I believe on theoretical grounds that allusions and the other types of intertextual reference discussed in chapter 1 are not hard, verifiable phenomena like species of bird, capable of being cataloged or tabulated. But even if we disregard the theoretical difficulties, the practical difficulty that remains—of deciding what does and does not deserve to be included—is almost insurmountable. Many of the citations of classical authors in the early commentaries seem to me to be grammatical precedents rather than allusive targets, but one cannot always be sure.

34. Riggs, in *Christian Poet in "Paradise Lost,"* argues that "the epic characters of Milton's poem are drawn with continued reference to the poet as he is portrayed in the four lyrical prologues" (p. 1); see especially Riggs's introduction, pp. 1–14, and pp. 178–82.

35. This is actually the first of four precedents that he cites; the others are Pollux, Theseus, and Hercules (6.121–23).

36. The analogy between Orpheus and the narrator of *Paradise Lost* has been noted before; see Allen, "Milton and the Descent to Light." On the figure of Orpheus generally, see Segal, *Orpheus: The Myth of the Poet*. Milton had brooded on this parallel between himself and Orpheus for a long time; see the excellent interpretation of *Lycidas* by J. Martin Evans, in *Cambridge Companion to Milton*, pp. 41–48.

37. McColley, *Milton's Technique of Source Adaptation*, pp. 1–32, shows that one of Milton's main techniques of verbal adaptation of a source passage, i.e., "reworking," is to imitate salient features of the source in reverse order. I have already suggested that this technique was learned from Vergil.

38. Blessington, *"Paradise Lost" and the Classical Epic*, p. 1, notes only that the council in hell in *Paradise Lost* 2 in certain respects re-

sembles *Iliad* 2.53–394. As for the council in heaven in *Paradise Lost* 3, Blessington (p. 37) refers only to the divine councils that occur in the first books of each of the three classical epics. It might be noted that Lewalski's argument concerning the epic structure of *Paradise Regained* is based upon observations concerning the heavenly councils in that poem; see Lewalski, *Milton's Brief Epic*, and Carey's summary of her argument in Carey and Fowler, p. 1065.

39. Rajan notes that when his scene is celestial, Milton eschews the typical embellishments of pagan epic: "According to my count, 2140 lines of *Paradise Lost* are set in Heaven. Yet in all these lines there is not a single complex or multiple simile, only one simile which involves a literary allusion, and only one place name, Biblical or classical" (*"Paradise Lost" and the Seventeenth Century Reader*, pp. 163–64, n. 26).

40. There is a small verbal link here: of Belial, Milton says that he is, "To vice industrious, but to nobler deeds / Timorous and slothful, yet he pleased the ear" (2.116–17), which resembles Vergil's equally unfavorable description of Drances, "largus opum et lingua melior, sed frigida bello / dextera" (11.338–39: "loose with his money and more so with his tongue, but with cold feet [literally, 'a cold right hand'] for war"). The comparison between Belial and Drances could be further elaborated.

41. Behind the simile at *Aeneid* 9.59–64 lie similes at *Argonautica* 1.1243–47, and *Odyssey* 6.130–34; cf. *Georgics* 3.537–38. John 10.1 provides the Biblical counterpoint.

42. Blessington often is looking for a particular detail and failing to see the whole; he is trying to find a parallel for Adam's attempt to keep Eve from going off on her own:

> For a classicist like Milton the most obvious parallel to the separation of Adam and Eve, a separation that brings on tragedy, was that of Dido and Aeneas, but Milton did not evoke that scene with any directness of allusion nor did he recast the departure of Odysseus from Aiaia or the arguments used to detain Hector from battle. (*"Paradise Lost" and the Classical Epic*, p. 57)

He proceeds to review Mueller's reference to Patroklos and Achilles, in *"Paradise Lost and the Iliad."*

43. This simile, like the simile in *Argonautica* 3.876–84, is based on *Odyssey* 6.102–8, where Nausicaa is likened to Artemis. See the excellent discussion of this simile in Pöschl, *Art of Vergil*, pp. 60–68.

44. Todd in *Poetical Works of John Milton* cites Horace, *Odes* 3.4.27, not as an allusion, but simply to illustrate a Latinism; but the contexts of the Vergilian and Miltonic lines are so apposite that it seems likely the link is intended. With my discussion in this paragraph compare Harding, *Club of Hercules*, pp. 87–89, who sees the association of Eve with Dido as discrediting both Eve and Adam.

45. The idea of the "sympathy of nature" is characteristically Vergilian and is especially common in the *Eclogues:* cf. for example 1.38–39, 5.27–28 and 62–64, 10.13–16; with the latter passage especially cf. *Lycidas* 39–41.

46. Hume saw in Milton's lines an allusion to Ovid, *Metamorphoses* 1, which he quotes thus (at 9.782):

—Totusque perhorruit Orbis
Attonitus tanto subitae terrore ruinae.

Ovid's lines actually run thus:

sic, cum manus inpia saeuit
sanguine Caesareo Romanum extinguere nomen,
attonitum tanto subitae terrore ruinae
humanum genus est totusque perhorruit orbis.

(*Metamorphoses* 1.200–3)

(Just so, when an impious band raged to destroy the Roman name with Caesar's death, the human race was astonished with great fear of sudden ruin and the entire globe shuddered.)

These lines constitute a historical simile describing the reaction of the assembled gods to Jupiter's disclosure of a plot against his rule devised by the mortal, Lycaon. The resemblance here to Milton's passage is limited to the last words, "totusque perhorruit orbis." The point in Milton is that the natural order reacted to Eve's sin, while "totus . . . orbis" in Ovid's lines is merely a metonymy for "people everywhere," a fact obscured by Hume's misquotation. And, in any case, "perhorruit" might better be referred to *Paradise Lost* 9.1000, "Earth trembled," than to 9.782, where Hume cites it.

47. There are about two dozen uses of the adjective "certus" in the *Aeneid*, but besides the two cited here, the only other use with a dependent dative or genitive occurs at 2.350, where the context is inapposite to Milton's uses. The text at *Aeneid* 2.349–50 is troubled; see R. D. Williams.

48. See the entry in Milton's Commonplace Book, *Complete Prose Works of John Milton*, ed. Wolfe, 1:420.

49. R. D. Williams at 286 glosses: "CAESAR hic est qui dicitur Gaius Iulius Caesar" ("CAESAR: this is the one who is called Gaius Julius Caesar"). "Iulius" is not a problem as it may refer equally well to Augustus, whose name after his adoption by his grand-uncle was Gaius Julius Caesar Octavianus. Vergil is linking the modern-day Julian *gens* with its eponymous heroic ancestor, so the "Iulius" is obviously required. As Williams points out, the reference to oriental spoils in line 289 fits Augustus better than Julius. Since lines 291–96 refer indubitably to Augustus, who was responsible for the closing of the temple of Janus in 29 B.C. (see Augustus' *Res Gestae* 13), if lines 286–88 do *not* refer to Augustus, the "tum" in 291 must convey the change of reference, which is highly unlikely. I am unaware of any evidence as to Milton's interpretation of the lines other than what can be inferred from the allusion.

50. See Porter, "Look at Vergil's Negative Image."

51. The argument of the last few pages was first briefly sketched in Porter, "Dancing around Milton's Allusions," especially pp. 170–72.

52. See Blessington, *"Paradise Lost" and the Classical Epic*. Blessington is one of the first modern commentators to read this association right-side-up. Others, such as Steadman (in book after book), kept insisting that the association was intended to discredit Aeneas, as if readers in the seventeenth century were quite ready to find Aeneas a figure of incarnate evil.

53. See 1.35, 3.553, 5.662, and 9.254: Satan envies both the Son, and Adam and Eve.

54. I am thinking, of course, of Stanley Fish's thesis in *Surprised by Sin:* that the reader is tricked into approving some evil that he or she must later repent .

55. I would not dare raise the question of *belief* anywhere but in a note, but it should perhaps be raised somewhere. Vergil's question— "tantaene animis caelestibus irae?—is surely meant to be strong, perhaps scandalous, especially if one thinks of all the worrying that Socrates does over Homer's imputation of malignancy to the gods. But can we respond feelingly to this line? After all, we reject his gods— and for that matter, he probably did, too. Gordon Williams (*Figures of Thought,* p. 213) puts things quite frankly:

> In my view, the text of the *Aeneid* enjoins a reading that is entirely consistent with the theology of Epicurus: death is the end of everything, and the gods, if they exist, are remote beings, possible objects of human contemplation, but without the slightest interest in the world of human beings and certainly never inclined to intervene in the world. The gods are a narrative device, a fiction of the poet, a synecdoche of human attempts to explain an essentially hostile universe that recognizes itself as a fiction and is subverted sufficiently often by the poet to maintain that fictionality.

I would like to disagree but cannot, and what is worse, I am inclined increasingly to think that Vergil has described my world as well as Williams has described Vergil's. At this point, the question begins to change. How many of us can respond feelingly to Milton's claim to "justify God's ways to men"?

Chapter 4
Quantum mutatus:
Language

1. Another famous mock-epic is the *Margites,* ascribed by a Byzantine scholiast to the same author as the *Batrachomyomachia.* Plato

(2 *Alcibiades* 147 a) quotes a hexameter verse from the work: πολλ᾽ ἠπίστατο ἔργα, κακῶς δ᾽ ἠπίστατο πάντα ("He knew how to do many deeds, but he knew how to do them badly"). Aristotle (*Poetics* 1448b) thought well of the work.

2. I refer readers who find the idea of translation within a single language perverse to George Steiner's *After Babel*, especially the first chapter.

3. It is likewise one of the very fundamental differences between the Old and New Testaments of the Bible that the Old Testament or Hebrew Bible was written largely in the language of its writers, while the New Testament was written in Greek, which for its authors was a learned second language.

4. This is a more complicated question than I am making it sound. In *Epistles* 2.3.47–58 (the *Ars Poetica*) Horace's view seems to be different. Even if that passage is ironic (as I suspect), it must be noted that we have a fragment of Lucilius himself criticizing the use of Greek words in conversation (87–93, in Lucilius, *Remains of Old Latin*, ed. Warmington). What is clear is that the texts of Horace and Vergil are much freer of foreign importations than those of Lucretius (who preceded) or Petronius and Apuleius (who followed).

5. See Cicero, *Brutus* 252–62, where Caesar's style is praised for its purity. At 262, Cicero notes that Caesar, in his own treatise on language (the *De analogia*) had said that "the choice of words is the beginning of eloquence" ("uerborum dilectum originem esse eloquentiae").

6. Corns, *Milton's Language*, pp. 88–89. Novel combinations of this sort are one of the ways for orators to embellish their language: see Cicero, *De oratore* 3.38.154.

7. Hunter, *Descent of Urania*, pp. 224–25. Hunter attributes this view to Henry Bradley, the great editor of the *Oxford English Dictionary*.

8. Hunter, *Descent of Urania*, p. 240.

9. Ennius' "horrentia tela uirorum" (*Annales* 285, in Ennius, *Remains of Old Latin*, ed. Warmington) is more likely to be Vergil's source

than Milton's, but Statius' "saeptum . . . horrentibus armis" (*Thebaid* 2.385: "fenced in with bristling arms") is more apposite to Milton's context than is Vergil's line.

10. It is just this sort of thing that is found so frequently in the early commentaries on *Paradise Lost*, and I am sure that the commentators are often citing what they would have thought as a grammatical (lexical) precedent rather than trying to identify a genuine allusion. When another language, such as Greek or Hebrew, lies behind the Latin, things can get very complicated indeed, and sensitive linguists can make gross mistakes. The English translator of Auerbach's *Literary Language and Its Public in Late Antiquity* mistranslates the phrase "de corpore mortis huius" from Augustine (actually from St. Paul via the Old Latin Bible) as "from the body of this death," which is nonsense, because he does not recognize that the Latin here is translating very literally from Greek, and the Greek is using a Hebraic or Aramaic idiom, the descriptive or appositive genitive: "de corpore huius mortis" = "from this mortal body." See Auerbach, *Literary Language*, p. 30; and Zerwick, *Biblical Greek*, §40, 41.

11. Leonard Welsted, "A Dissertation concerning the Perfection of the *English* Language, the State of Poetry, etc.," in *Epistles, Odes, &c.* (1724), ix; quoted in *Milton: The Critical Heritage*, ed. Shawcross, p. 244.

12. This is an estimate, but, I think, an accurate one. Sixteen of the eighteen volumes of the Columbia *Works of John Milton*, ed. Patterson, are dedicated to Milton's prose (vols. 3–18); since volume 3 contains two parts, we might grant seventeen volumes to the prose. Of these, ten and a half are taken up with works in Latin, including the *Defensio Prima* and the *Defensio Secunda*, the *Pro Se Defensio, Logica*, the Prolusions, the vast bulk of his correspondence both personal and formal, the state papers, and, finally, the *De Doctrina Christiana*, which in itself occupies four volumes. Of course, the Latin works are accompanied by translations (sometimes quite inaccurate), but many of these volumes are rather more bulky than most of the English volumes.

13. Not much is known about Dobson himself. The title page of his translation declares that he held the LL.B. (baccalaureate of letters) from New College, Oxford. The first volume of the translation was dedicated to William Benson (1682–1754), a patron of literature and a special admirer of Milton; it was he who erected the monument to Milton in Westminster Abbey in 1737. *The Dictionary of National Biography*, which does not contain an article on Dobson, does mention in its article on Benson that he gave Dobson £1000 to translate *Paradise Lost* into Latin verse. Benson also admired Vergil greatly. He published a couple of essays on aspects of Vergil's poetry, and he encouraged Christopher Pitt's translation of the *Aeneid*. Fifty-six lines from the opening of Dobson's version of book 3 appeared in *The Museum*, vol. 2, no. 16, in 1746, with a short prefatory note by someone identifying himself only by the initials "A. B.," referring to Dobson's translation as a work "preparing for the Press" and one "which the Publick has great Expectations from" (p. 98). Sometime after the completion of his translation of Milton, Dobson published a short narrative poem in English titled *The Prussian Campaign*. The publication is not dated, but the subtitle states the poem's concern with "The Atchievements of Frederick the Great, in the Years 1756–57." Dobson eschews rhyme, following Milton's example rather than the prevailing practice of his own day. It is a rather bad poem.

14. *Paradisus Amissus.* / Poema / Joannis Miltoni / Latine Redditum / a Guilielmo Dobson, LL.B. / Nov. Coll. Oxon. Socio., in two volumes: Oxonii, / e Theatro Sheldoniano, / MDCCL [vol. 1, containing books. 1–6]; and Londini, / Typis Jacobi Bettenham. / MDCCLIII [vol. 2, containing books. 7–12]. References here to Dobson's translation are to volume and page of the complete edition. It was my extraordinary good fortune to discover, after I had decided I needed to examine Dobson's version, that one of the few copies of the book in the United States was in Houston, in the rare books room of the Fondren Library at Rice University.

15. On the old lie that Latin is inherently more economical than English, see the illuminating remarks of Guy Lee, appended to his translation of Ovid's *Amores*, pp. 205–7.

16. Prince's description of Milton's prosody in *The Italian Element in Milton's Verse* still seems the best to me.

17. Among the best comments on this much-commented-upon trick is that of Christopher Ricks in *Milton's Grand Style*, pp. 109–17.

18. Quoted in Perosa and Sparrow, *Renaissance Latin Verse: An Anthology*, p. 247. Their text is based on sixteenth-century editions of Vida. It is worth noting that Vida's *De Arte Poetica* had been translated into English in 1725 by Christopher Pitt, the translator of Vergil, who, like Dobson, enjoyed the patronage of George Benson.

19. "Noxa" is glossed by the *Oxford Latin Dictionary* as "injurious behaviour" or "wrongdoing." It was also the choice of several other translators of *Paradise Lost*, the first being Thomas Powers, whose version of book 1 appeared in 1691. In my attempt to render the proem, I chose "seditio," but I freely admit its inadequacy, too.

20. W. Leonard Grant, *Neo-Latin Literature and the Pastoral*, p. 47. Quint (*Origin and Originality*, p. 78) quotes a pertinent remark from Erasmus' *Ciceronianus:* "Pie [pia materia] tractari qui potest, si nunquam dimoueas oculos a Virgiliis, Oratiis, ac Nasonibus?" ("How can pious material be handled in a pious manner if you never take your eyes off Vergils or Horaces or Ovids?").

21. Fantazzi, "Making of the *De Partu Virginis*," pp. 129, 128, respectively.

22. Quint, *Origin and Originality*, p. 78.

23. Fantazzi, "Making of the *De Partu Virginis*," p. 131.

24. Quotations from the (Clementine) Vulgate and Greek New Testament here and elsewhere are from the critical edition of Merk, *Novum Testamentum Graece et Latine*.

25. Cf. Job 28.28, "timor Domini, ipsa est sapientia" ("The fear of the Lord is wisdom itself").

26. Auerbach, *Mimesis*, p. 48.

27. Auerbach, *Mimesis*, p. 74.

28. Auerbach, *Mimesis*, p. 75.

29. Fantazzi, "Making of the *De Partu Virginis*," p. 130.

30. Porter, translator's preface to "Eclogue Five of Mantuan," pp. 7–8.

31. Very fortunate, this, as there are in the end differences, and the production of such a dictionary would entail facing some extraordinarily subtle semantic problems.

32. Rand, "Milton in Rustication," p. 111.

33. "Cuium" in *Eclogue* 3.1 is, I think, a deliberate and comic oddity. T. E. Page notes that the word was "common in the early comedians but obsolete in Virgil's day in formal Latin."

34. Auerbach, *Mimesis*, p. 31.

35. W. R. Johnson, *Idea of Lyric*, p. 172.

36. A few years after its original publication in London, Hog's version was republished in Amsterdam. Jean Gillet surmises that it must have been the version by means of which Voltaire, who knew no English, first became acquainted with the poem, although, Gillet adds, "le texte de Hog ne lui aurait donnée qu'une idée bien mutilée du poème" (*Le "Paradise Perdu" dans la litterature française*, p. 41).

Appendix

1. According to Edward Phillips, Milton's nephew and biographer, certain lines of Satan's address to the Sun at the beginning of book 4 were originally written and seen by him years earlier, as the opening verses of the planned tragedy. Aside from this brief passage (Phillips speaks of "six verses" but quotes ten; see his "Life of Milton," appended to *Complete Poems and Major Prose*, ed. Hughes, pp. 1034–35), there is no evidence of significant portions of the epic having been originally drafted for the drama. Composition of the epic began sometime in the late 1650s; the exact date is disputed.

2. Milton refers to his planned Arthurian epic in *Mansus* 80–84, in the *Epitaphium Damonis* 162–78, and in the Trinity manuscript. As Milton's career is a prime example of the Vergilian progression from pastoral to epic, it is interesting to note that Vergil himself seems to have considered writing a historical epic, perhaps in the manner of Ennius. Could it be that Milton, consciously or not, flirted with the Arthurian idea because it was part of the role that he had fashioned for himself as a Vergilian *uates*?

3. Epic theory was closely associated with dramatic theory in the Renaissance, on the strength of Aristotle's recommendation in chap. 23 of the *Poetics* that the epic plot should be constructed on dramatic principles. See Steadman, *Epic and Tragic Structure*, and Gardner, "Milton's 'Satan.'"

4. Gardner, "Milton's 'Satan,'" pp. 213–14.

5. In addition, the argument to book 12 was slightly altered. The arguments, not present in the original printing of 1667, were added in the 1668 printing, along with the note on the verse, but until the 1674 second edition, all the arguments were printed together before the poem, instead of before the individual books.

6. See the introduction in Hughes, pp. 173–77, and Barker, "Structural Pattern."

7. See Barker, "Structural Pattern," p. 151. According to Barker, Milton was not content to eat his cake: he had to have it, too. A five-act structure is still present in 1674, but now one of the acts, the third, occupies four books (5 through 8) instead of two. "The dramatic and epic structural patterns are thus brought into exact alignment by the simple redivision of 1674. *Paradise Lost* is in fact the consummate example of five-act epic structure" (p. 153). But Barker is hungry for cake, too, and we are soon told: "If the disposition of the masses was patient of a tragic pattern of structural interpretation in 1667, the unmoved masses remain patient of it after the tinkering of 1674. . . . One must read both poems and see both patterns" (p. 154). I know that some of my readers will think that I am asking a lot when I suggest that we need to read both *Paradise Lost* and the *Aeneid* carefully together, but at least I am only asking that we read one version of each poem. The continued description of the poem of 1674 in terms of "five-act" structure is sheer wilfulness. Unless one is willing to resurrect Davenant's *Gondibert* (to which Barker refers as an authoritative precedent, pp. 147–48) to higher esteem than posterity has hitherto accorded it, we shall have few other poems to include in the class of five-act epics of which *Paradise Lost* is the "consummation." I grant that the *faux pas* of the 1667 edition is embarrassing, but there is no

shortage of evidence that poets will sweat blood over single lines or even single words, so we should not regard what Milton did in 1674 as "tinkering."

8. See Martz, *Milton: Poet of Exile*, pp. 158, 160, for sensible criticisms of the five-act hypothesis.

9. The most elaborate exposition of the numerological patterns is by Qvarnstrom, *Enchanted Palace;* see especially chap. 2, "The Christocentric Structure." See also Whaler's epilogue to *Counterpoint and Symbol;* he sees the tetrachys in *Paradise Lost* differently, as a descending progression of groups of books (4, 3, 2, 1). A summary of less controversial points, including the theory of the "tetrachys," is to be found in Fowler's introduction, pp. 440–43. Anthony Low summarizes Milton's interest in the same arithmetic or numerological pattern in *Paradise Regained,* where the three temptations of Christ in the Bible are expanded to ten and distributed in parcels of one, two, three, and four temptations, respectively throughout the four books of Milton's brief epic; see *Georgic Revolution,* p. 337, and further references there.

10. In the first edition, books 1 through 6 comprised 5426 lines, and the remaining four books comprised 5124 lines. Does it matter that the lines of the first edition were numbered, but very haphazardly?

11. Fowler says that "the extreme length of *Ed I* Bk x . . . certainly suggests that the subsequent division was planned from the start" (*Poems of John Milton,* ed. Carey and Fowler, p. 442).

12. Incidentally, Martz's claim (p. 160) that "the *Lusiad* is the only important epic before *Paradise Lost* that was thus divided into ten parts" is in error. Lucan's *Bellum Ciuile* also has ten books (the last unfinished) and for thematic reasons would have been much more interesting to Milton than Camoëns. Lucan's importance for Milton is a subject deserving further study.

13. Summers, *Muse's Method,* p. 112.

14. James Joyce provides an ironic parallel. As Vladimir Nabokov observes, "Joyce himself very soon realized with dismay that the

harping on those essentially easy and vulgar 'Homeric parallelisms'
would only distract one's attention from the real beauty of his book.
He soon dropped these pretentious chapter titles which already were
'explaining' the book to non-readers" (*Strong Opinions*, p. 90; from
an interview conducted in 1966 and first printed in *Wisconsin Studies
in Contemporary Literature* 8 [1967]).

Works Cited

A Note on Primary Texts

I have made frequent reference to early commentaries on *Paradise Lost*, especially the first full commentary on the entire poem, by Patrick Hume (1695); the first variorum edition of Milton's poetry, edited by Bishop Thomas Newton (1749); and the second variorum, by the Reverend Henry J. Todd (1st ed., 1809). In general, Hume, Newton, and other contributors to the first and second variorums (Stillingfleet and Thyer) are quoted out of Todd's comprehensive commentary in its fifth edition (*Poetical Works of John Milton*, London, 1852). For information about these men and the early commentaries, see Ants Oras, *Milton's Editors and Commentators*, especially chapter 13.

Whenever possible, citations of classical works are in standard format and readers can track down a reference in any decent edition that is handy. Nonclassicists will probably find it most convenient to refer to the texts in the Loeb Classical Library; many of the older volumes in this series give outdated texts and vicious translations, but they can be serviceable nonetheless, and some of the more recent editions have been excellent. For further basic information about texts, translations, and critical studies, I recommend *The Cambridge History of Classical Literature*, edited by P. E. Easterling and E. J. Kenney, which provides short bibliographies for all the major classical authors. My quotations of classical texts have been checked against the modern critical editions, but are often slightly synthetic. (Most notable: capitalization has been reduced to a minimum, and in Latin, *u* replaces older *v*, so *revocare* becomes *reuocare*. These minor modifications are made in deference to the authority of the *Oxford Latin Dictionary* and contemporary conventions among classicists.) Quotations from Neo-Latin, on the other hand, are given exactly as found in my texts. I should note that the classical Greek and Latin texts quoted so frequently in the early commentaries on Milton's poetry do not always agree with what you will find in more recent editions of the classics. The disagreements, however, are usually trivial, and I have commented upon them in only a few cases where it seemed especially pertinent. Unless otherwise noted, all translations are my own.

Milton's texts present less difficult problems. The English prose is quoted from the Yale edition of Don M. Wolfe (*Complete Prose Works of John Milton*), but since Wolfe does not include the Latin works in Latin, my few quotations from the Latin prose are taken from the Columbia edition of Milton's entire works edited by F. A. Patterson (*Works of John Milton*). These sources are cited in the body of the text as "Wolfe" and "Patterson" respectively, followed by volume and page references. Poetry is quoted from the edition of John Carey and Alastair Fowler (*Poems of John Milton*); Fowler is responsible for *Paradise Lost*. Their commentary is more sensitive to the classical parallels than that of Merritt Y. Hughes (*Complete Poems and Major Prose*); and besides, I prefer their regularized, modern orthography to the regularized, seventeenth-century text of Hughes, which throws so much emphasis on the look of the words printed on the page. You cannot really begin to appreciate Miltonic intertextuality until you have gotten a fair bit of both Milton and the classics off the page and into your head.

Citations for quotations of primary texts have usually been provided in the body of the chapters, directly following the quotation. In a few places I have included an editor's name, to obviate confusion about the source.

What follows here is merely a list of secondary (and a few primary) works cited in the notes. I have learned much from many, but a list of all the works I myself have consulted in the course of this short study would be disproportionately—and pointlessly—long. More information, at least regarding work done in the last few years, can be found in the bibliographies compiled by the Institute for the Classical Tradition at Boston University and published annually by the journal *Classical and Modern Literature*.

References

Adams, R. M. *Milton and the Modern Critics*. Ithaca: Cornell University Press, 1965.

Addison, Joseph. *The Spectator* 369 (3 May 1712). Quoted in *Milton: The Critical Heritage*, edited by John T. Shawcross, p. 219. New York: Barnes and Noble, 1970.

Allen, Don Cameron. "Milton and the Descent to Light." In *Milton: Modern Essays in Criticism*, edited by A. E. Barker, pp. 177–95. New York: Oxford University Press, 1965.

Anderson, William S. "Vergil's Second *Iliad*." *TAPA* 88 (1957): 17–30.

Armour, Peter. "Dante's Virgil." In *Virgil in a Cultural Tradition*, edited by R. A. Cardwell and J. Hamilton, pp. 65–76. University of Nottingham Monographs in the Humanities, 4. Nottingham, 1986.

Auerbach, Erich. *Literary Language and Its Public in Latin Antiquity*. Translated by Ralph Manheim. New York: Pantheon Books, 1965.

———. *Mimesis: The Representation of Reality in Western Literature*. Translated by Willard R. Trask. Princeton: Princeton University Press, 1953.

Barker, A. E. "Structural Pattern in *Paradise Lost*." *Philological Quarterly* 28 (1949): 16–30. Reprinted in *Milton: Modern Essays in Criticism*, edited by A. E. Barker, pp. 142–55. New York: Oxford University Press, 1965.

———, ed. *Milton: Modern Essays in Criticism*. New York: Oxford University Press, 1965.

Blessington, Francis C. *"Paradise Lost" and the Classical Epic*. Boston: Routledge and Kegan Paul, 1979.

Bowra, C. M. *Pindar*. Oxford: Clarendon Press, 1964.

Bush, Douglas. "Virgil and Milton." *Classical Journal* 47 (1952): 178–82, 203–4.

Callimachus. Edited by C. A. Trypanis. Loeb Classical Library. Cambridge: Harvard University Press, 1958.

Campbell, David A., ed. *Greek Lyric.* 4 vols. Loeb Classical Library. Cambridge: Harvard University Press, 1982.

Camps, W. A. *An Introduction to Virgil's "Aeneid."* London: Oxford University Press, 1969.

Cardwell, R. A., and J. Hamilton, eds. *Virgil in a Cultural Tradition.* University of Nottingham Monographs in the Humanities, 4. Nottingham, 1986.

Carey, John, ed. See Milton, *The Poems of John Milton.*

Chapman, George. *Chapman's Homer.* Edited by Allardyce Nicoll. Bollingen Series, 41. 2d ed. Princeton: Princeton University Press, 1967.

Colie, Rosalie L. *The Resources of Kind.* Berkeley and Los Angeles: University of California Press, 1973.

Commager, Steele. *The Odes of Horace: A Critical Study.* Bloomington: Indiana University Press, 1962.

Condee, Ralph Waterbury. *Structure in Milton's Poetry: From the Foundation to the Pinnacles.* University Park: Pennsylvania State University Press, 1974.

Conte, Gian Biagio. *The Rhetoric of Imitation: Genre and Poetic Memory in Virgil and Other Latin Poets.* Translated by Charles Segal. Ithaca: Cornell University Press, 1986.

Corns, Thomas N. *Milton's Language.* Oxford: Basil Blackwell, 1990.

Crump, Galbraith M., ed. *Approaches to Teaching Milton's "Paradise Lost."* New York: Modern Language Association of America, 1986.

Curtius, Ernst Robert. *European Literature and the Latin Middle Ages.* Translated by Willard R. Trask. Princeton: Princeton University Press, 1953.

Dryden, John. *The Poems and Fables of John Dryden.* Edited by James Kinsley. 1962, Reprint. New York: Oxford University Press, 1970.

DuRocher, Richard J. *Milton and Ovid*. Ithaca: Cornell University
      Press, 1985.
Easterling, P. E., and E. J. Kenney, eds. *The Cambridge History of Clas-
      sical Literature*. 2 vols. Cambridge: Cambridge University Press,
      1982–85.
Eliot, T. S. *Complete Poems and Selected Plays*. New York: Harcourt
      Brace Jovanovich, 1971.
————. *Selected Essays*. Rev. ed. New York: Harcourt, Brace and
      World, 1964.
[Ennius.] *Remains of Old Latin*. Edited and translated by E. H.
      Warmington. Vol. 1. Loeb Classical Library. Cambridge: Har-
      vard University Press, 1979.
Evans, J. Martin. "*Lycidas*." In *The Cambridge Companion to Milton*,
      edited by Dennis Danielson, pp. 35–50. Cambridge: Cambridge
      University Press, 1989.
Fantazzi, Charles. "The Making of *De Partu Virginis*." In *Acta Con-
      ventus Neo-Latini Sanctandreani: Proceedings of the Fifth Interna-
      tional Congress of Neo-Latin Studies*, edited by I. D. McFarlane, pp.
      127–34. Binghamton, N.Y.: Medieval and Renaissance Texts
      and Studies, 1986.
Finley, J. H., Jr. "Milton and Horace: A Study of Milton's Sonnets."
      Harvard Studies in Classical Philology 48 (1937): 29–73.
Fish, Stanley. *Surprised by Sin: The Reader in "Paradise Lost."* New
      York: Macmillan, 1967.
Fowler, Alastair, ed. See Milton, *The Poems of John Milton*.
Gadamer, Hans-Georg. "Composition and Interpretation." In
      The Relevance of the Beautiful and Other Essays, edited by Robert
      Bernasconi. New York: Cambridge University Press, 1986.
Gallagher, Philip J. "*Paradise Lost*" and the Greek Theogony."
      English Literary Renaissance 9 (1979): 121–48.
Gardner, Helen. "Milton's 'Satan' and the Theme of Damnation
      in Elizabethan Tragedy." In *Milton: Modern Essays in Criticism*,
      edited by A. E. Barker, pp. 205–17. New York: Oxford Univer-
      sity Press, 1965.

Gilbert, A. H., ed. and trans. *Literary Criticism: Plato to Dryden*. Detroit: Wayne State University Press, 1962.

Gillet, Jean. *Le "Paradise Perdu" dans la litterature française*. Paris: Klincksieck, 1975.

Grant, W. Leonard. *Neo-Latin Literature and the Pastoral*. Chapel Hill: University of North Carolina Press, 1965.

Harding, Davis P. *The Club of Hercules: Studies in the Classical Background of "Paradise Lost."* Illinois Studies in Language and Literature, vol. 50. Urbana: University of Illinois Press, 1962.

———. *Milton and the Renaissance Ovid*. Urbana: University of Illinois Press, 1946.

Herrick, Robert. *The Poetical Works of Robert Herrick*. Edited by L. C. Martin. Oxford: Clarendon Press, 1956.

Hesiod. *Theogony*. Edited by M. L. West. Oxford: Clarendon Press, 1966.

Hollander, John. *The Figure of Echo: A Mode of Allusion in Milton and After*. Berkeley and Los Angeles: University of California Press, 1981.

Horace. *A Commentary on Horace: Odes, Book II*. Edited by R. G. M. Nisbet and Margaret Hubbard. Oxford: Clarendon Press, 1978.

———. *The Odes*. Edited by Kenneth Quinn. London: Macmillan, 1980.

Hughes, Merritt Y. "Milton's Celestial Battle and the Theogonies." In *Ten Perspectives on Milton*, pp. 196–219. New Haven: Yale University Press, 1965.

———, ed. See Milton, *Complete Poems and Major Prose*.

Hume, Patrick. *Annotations on Milton's "Paradise Lost."* London, 1695. Reprint. London: Folcroft Library Editions, 1971.

Hunter, W. B. *The Descent of Urania: Studies in Milton, 1946–1988*. Lewisburg, Penn.: Bucknell University Press, 1989.

Johnson, Samuel. *Lives of the English Poets* [Cowley to Prior]. Garden City, N.Y.: Doubleday, n.d.

Johnson, W. R. *The Idea of Lyric: Lyric Modes in Ancient and Modern Poetry*. Berkeley and Los Angeles: University of California Press, 1982.

————. *Momentary Monsters: Lucan and His Heroes.* Ithaca: Cornell University Press, 1987.

Kennedy, George. *The Art of Rhetoric in the Roman World, 300 B.C.–A.D. 300.* Princeton: Princeton University Press, 1972.

Kerrigan, William. *The Prophetic Milton.* Charlottesville: University of Virginia Press, 1974.

Knauer, Georg Nicolaus. *Die "Aeneis" und Homer: Studien zur poetischen Technik Vergils mit Listen der Homerzitate in der "Aeneis."* Hypomnemata, 7. Göttingen: Vandenhoeck and Ruprecht, 1964.

————. "Vergil's *Aeneid* and Homer." *Greek, Roman and Byzantine Studies* 5 (1964): 61–84.

Labriola, Albert C. "The Titans and the Giants: *Paradise Lost* and the Tradition of the Renaissance Ovid." *Milton Quarterly* 12 (1978): 9–16.

Lanham, Richard A. *A Handlist of Rhetorical Terms.* Berkeley and Los Angeles: University of California Press, 1969.

Lewalski, Barbara Kiefer. "The Genres of *Paradise Lost.*" In *The Cambridge Companion to Milton,* edited by Dennis Danielson, pp. 79–95. Cambridge: Cambridge University Press, 1989.

————. *Milton's Brief Epic.* Providence: Brown University Press, 1966.

————. *"Paradise Lost" and the Rhetoric of Literary Forms.* Princeton: Princeton University Press, 1985.

Lewis, C. S. *Preface to "Paradise Lost."* London: Oxford University Press, 1942.

Low, Anthony. *The Georgic Revolution.* Princeton: Princeton University Press, 1985.

[Lucilius.] *Remains of Old Latin.* Edited and translated by E. H. Warmington. Vol. 3. Loeb Classical Library. Cambridge: Harvard University Press, 1979.

Lyne, R. O. A. M. *Futher Voices in Vergil's "Aeneid."* Oxford: Clarendon Press, 1987.

Martz, Louis L. *Milton: Poet of Exile.* 2d ed. New Haven: Yale University Press, 1986.

McColley, Grant. *Milton's Technique of Source Adaptation*. Chapel Hill: University of North Carolina Press, 1938.

Merk, Augustinus, ed. *Novum Testamentum Graece et Latine*. Rome: Pontifical Biblical Institute, 1964.

Milton, John. *Complete Poems and Major Prose*. Edited by Merritt Y. Hughes. New York: Odyssey Press, 1957.

———. *Complete Prose Works of John Milton*. Edited by Don M. Wolfe. 8 vols. New Haven: Yale University Press, 1953–82.

———. *Paradise Lost, 1667*. Scolar Press Facsimile. Menston, Eng.: Scolar Press, 1968.

———. *Paradisus Amissus*. Translated by William Dobson. 2 vols. Oxford and London, 1750, 1753.

———. *The Poems of John Milton*. Edited and with commentary by John Carey and Alastair Fowler. Longman's Annotated English Poets. London and New York: Longman, 1968.

———. [Second Variorum] *Poetical Works of John Milton, with Notes of Various Authors*. Edited by Henry John Todd. 4 vols. 5th ed. London, 1852.

———. *The Works of John Milton*. Edited by F. A. Patterson. New York: Columbia University Press, 1931.

Minton, William W. "Homer's Invocations of the Muses: Traditional Patterns." *TAPA* 91 (1960): 292–309.

Mueller, Martin. "*Paradise Lost* and the *Iliad*." *Comparative Literature Studies* 6 (1969): 292–316.

Nabokov, Vladimir. *Strong Opinions*. New York: Vintage International, 1990.

Newman, John Kevin. *The Classical Epic Tradition*. Wisconsin Studies in the Classics, edited by B. H. Fowler and W. G. Moon. Madison: University of Wisconsin Press, 1986.

Newton, Thomas, ed., first variorum edition of Milton's poetry (1749). See Milton, [Second Variorum] *Poetical Works of John Milton*.

Oras, Ants. *Milton's Editors and Commentators from Patrick Hume to Henry John Todd (1695–1801)*. Rev. ed. New York: Oxford University Press, 1968.

Otis, Brooks. *Virgil: A Study in Civilised Poetry*. Oxford: Clarendon Press, 1963.

Ovid. *Amores*. Translated by Guy Lee. New York: Viking Press, 1968.

Patrick, J. Max, and Roger H. Sundell, eds. *Milton and the Art of Sacred Song*. Madison: University of Wisconsin Press, 1979.

Patrides, C. A., ed. *Approaches to "Paradise Lost": The York Tercentenary Lectures*. Toronto: University of Toronto Press, 1968.

Patterson, F. A., ed. See Milton, *The Works of John Milton*.

Perosa, A., and J. Sparrow, eds. *Renaissance Latin Verse: An Anthology*. Chapel Hill: University of North Carolina Press, 1979.

Porter, William M. Translator's preface to "Eclogue Five of Mantuan (1448–1516). *Candidus: On the Treatment of Poets by the Wealthy*." *Allegorica* 6 (1981): 7 8.

———. "Dancing around Milton's Allusions." In *Approaches to Teaching Milton's "Paradise Lost,"* edited by Galbraith M. Crump, pp. 165–75. New York: Modern Language Association of America, 1986.

———. "A Look at Vergil's Negative Image." *Arion* 3 (1976): 493–506.

Pöschl, Viktor. *The Art of Vergil: Image and Symbol in the "Aeneid."* Translated by G. Seligson. Ann Arbor: University of Michigan Press, 1962.

Prince, F. T. *The Italian Element in Milton's Verse*. Oxford: Clarendon Press, 1962.

Pucci, Pietro. *Hesiod and the Language of Poetry*. Baltimore: Johns Hopkins University Press, 1977.

Quint, David. *Origin and Originality in Renaissance Literature: Versions of the Source*. New Haven: Yale University Press, 1983.

Qvarnstrom, Gunnar. *The Enchanted Palace*. Stockholm: Almqvist and Wiksell, 1967.

Rajan, B. *"Paradise Lost" and the Seventeenth Century Reader*. Ann Arbor: University of Michigan Press, 1967.

Rand, Edward Kennard. "Milton in Rustication." *Studies in Philology* 19 (1922): 109–35.

Revard, Stella Purce. "Milton's Muse and the Daughters of Mem-
ory." *English Literary Renaissance* 9 (1979): 432–41.
————. *The War in Heaven: "Paradise Lost" and the Tradition of Satan's
Rebellion.* Ithaca: Cornell University Press, 1980.
Ricks, Christopher. *Milton's Grand Style.* Oxford: Clarendon Press,
1963.
Riggs, William G. *The Christian Poet in "Paradise Lost."* Berkeley and
Los Angeles: University of California Press, 1972.
Sannazaro, Jacopo. *De Partu Virginis.* Edited by Antonio Altamura.
Naples: Gaspare Casella, 1948.
Sasek, Lawrence A. "The Drama of *Paradise Lost,* Books XI and
XII." In *Milton: Modern Essays in Criticism,* edited by A. E. Barker,
pp. 342–45. New York: Oxford University Press, 1965.
Segal, Charles. *Orpheus: The Myth of the Poet.* Baltimore: Johns Hop-
kins University Press, 1988.
Servius. *Servianorum in Vergilii Carmina Commentariorum Editio Har-
vardiana.* Edited by E. K. Rand, J. J. Savage, et al. Vol. 2. Lan-
caster, Penn.: American Philological Association, 1946.
Shawcross, John T., ed. *Milton: The Critical Heritage.* New York:
Barnes and Noble, 1970.
Spenser, T. J. B. "*Paradise Lost:* The Anti-Epic." In *Approaches to
"Paradise Lost": The York Tercentenary Lectures,* edited by C. A.
Patrides, pp. 81–98. Toronto: University of Toronto Press, 1968.
Stanford, W. B. *The Ulysses Theme: A Study in the Adaptability of a
Traditional Hero.* 2d ed. Ann Arbor: University of Michigan
Press, 1968.
Steadman, John M. *Epic and Tragic Structure in "Paradise Lost."* Chi-
cago: University of Chicago Press, 1976.
————. *Milton and the Renaissance Hero.* Oxford: Clarendon Press,
1967.
————. *Milton's Epic Characters: Image and Idol.* Chapel Hill: Univer-
sity of North Carolina Press, 1968.
Steiner, George. *After Babel: Aspects of Language and Translation.*
London and New York: Oxford University Press, 1975.

Summers, Joseph. *The Muse's Method*. Cambridge: Harvard University Press, 1962.

Sundell, Roger H. "The Singer and His Song in the Prologues of *Paradise Lost*." In *Milton and the Art of Sacred Song*, edited by J. Max Patrick and Roger H. Sundell, pp. 65–80. Madison: University of Wisconsin Press, 1979.

Taylor, George C. *Milton's Use of Du Bartas*. Cambridge: Harvard University Press, 1934.

Tillyard, E. M. W. *The English Epic and its Background*. New York: Oxford University Press, 1954.

Todd, Henry John, ed. See Milton, [Second Variorum] *Poetical Works of John Milton*.

Virgil [P. Vergilius Maro]. *The Aeneid of Virgil*. Edited by R. D. Williams. London: Macmillan, 1975.

———. *Aeneidos Liber Sextus*. Edited by R. G. Austin. Oxford: Clarendon Press, 1977.

———. *Bucolica et Georgica*. Edited by T. E. Page. New York: St. Martin's Press, 1965.

Webber, Joan Malory. *Milton and His Epic Tradition*. Seattle: University of Washington Press, 1979.

Whaler, James. *Counterpoint and Symbol: An Inquiry into the Rhythm of Milton's Epic Style*. Anglistica 6. Copenhagen: Rosenkilde and Bagger, 1956.

Wigodsky, Mark. *Vergil and Early Latin Poetry*. Wiesbaden: Franz Steiner Verlag, 1972.

Willey, Basil. *The Seventeenth Century Background*. Garden City, N.Y.: Doubleday, 1953.

Williams, Gordon. *Figures of Thought in Roman Poetry*. New Haven: Yale University Press, 1980.

———. *Tradition and Originality in Roman Poetry*. Oxford: Clarendon Press, 1968.

Wolfe, Don M., ed. See Milton, *Complete Prose Works of John Milton*.

Zerwick, M. *Biblical Greek*. Rome: Pontifical Biblical Institute, 1963.

Index